Living by Faith
Dying with Hope

A Nurse's Story

Author: Kim Armstrong

Copyright © 2009 by Kim Armstrong

Living by Faith Dying with Hope
A Nurse's Story
by Kim Armstrong

Printed in the United States of America

ISBN 978-1-60791-621-5

All rights reserved solely by the author. The author guarantees all contents are original and do not infringe upon the legal rights of any other person or work. No part of this book may be reproduced in any form without the permission of the author. The views expressed in this book are not necessarily those of the publisher.

Unless otherwise indicated, Bible quotations are taken from The King James Version of the Bible (Thompson Chain-Reference Edition). Copyright © 1988 by B.B. Kirkbride Bible Company, Inc.

www.xulonpress.com

Acknowledgments

Many thanks to Mary Edwards and Erin Howarth from Detroit, MI. If it were not for you two special ladies, I would never have finished the first book. A special thanks to Alitza Aguirre and Elizabeth Witt for your copy editing and proofreading talents. I want to say thank you to Taylor, my sweet daughter, for giving me the perfect picture. Most importantly, I thank God for inspiration and courage to move outside the box.

Table of Contents

1. The Nurse 15
2. Shawn 19
3. Liaison 25
4. Suicide 33
5. Choices 43
6. Friend 51
7. Humility 57
8. Afterlife 61
9. Death's Sting 65
10. Lazarus 71
11. Rhea 77
12. Divine Appointment 83
13. My Healing 91
14. Defying Death 99
15. Dysfunctional 103
16. Special Needs 109
17. Never Give Up 115
18. Dad 119
19. Obedience 127
20. Mary 131

21. Tammie 139
22. Addictions 143
23. Death 149
24. Walls 153
25. Charlie 159
26. Futility 163
27. Freedom to Hope 167
28. Hell Night 173
29. Love Thy Neighbor 179
30. The Valley 185
31. Changed 189
32. Voices 193
33. A Mother's Hope 199
34. Ask and You Shall Receive 203
35. Attacks 207
36. Hope 211

―∞―

This paragraph was typed onto a small scrap of paper and handed to my friend Karen. She had just pronounced an elderly gentleman who had passed away during the evening hours. He was surrounded by a family who loved him dearly. As Karen tried to comfort those left behind, she was handed the following by one of the family members.

DEATH IS NOTHING AT ALL - - - I have only slipped away into the next room. Whatever we were to each other, that we are still. Call me by my old familiar name, speak to me in the easy way which you always used. Laugh as we always laughed together. Play, smile, think of me, pray for me. Let my name be the household word that it always was. Let it be spoken without effort. Life means all that it ever meant. It is the same as it ever was; there is absolutely unbroken continuity. Why should I be out of your mind because I am out of your sight? I am but waiting for you, for an interval, somewhere very near just around the corner. All is well. Nothing is past; nothing is lost. One brief moment and all will be as it was before - - only better, infinitely happier and forever - - - we will all be one together with Christ. ...Carmelite Monastery, Tallow County, Waterford, Ireland

Introduction

This collection of stories tells about God's miraculous intervention in seemingly hopeless situations. Some of the patients were rescued from a near death experience. Some were not. During their last struggling moments of life, many of the characters in this book were forced to accept the inevitable . . . death. Many faced their last days on earth not in fear and distress as one might expect, but with peace and dignity. They seemed certain that what awaited them after they breathed their last breath was not to be feared. These patients passed from this life into the next gently and peacefully. Some had questions about what awaited them. Most were sad to leave their loved ones behind. But many had suffered pain and sorrow to the point that they were ready to let go of life and move on to the eternal.

Terminal illness brings patients to the inevitable crossroads in life. People who face imminent death must decide which path they will walk. Do they hold onto faith and continue to hope for a miracle?

Do they hold onto the hope and belief that death is but a stepping stone from this mortal existence to eternal life with Christ? Or do they ignore Christ's promise of eternal life and leave this life, hopeless, with only the belief that death is final?

In the story "Suicide," you will read about people who hope for nothing but everlasting sleep in the grave. Their story leaves us with an aching feeling that can best be described as hopelessness. These young people thought that after death they would finally be at peace but this is not what God's word tells us will happen. God has given us the choice of eternal life with Him or eternal punishment in Hell. Many people who are facing death are given the chance to hear about God and His love for them regardless of how they lived their life. He beckons them and gives them a chance to know Him, even when death hovers so close. This acceptance of Christ and eternal life is the Hope that Christians have as they face their own imminent death. It is this Hope that brings peace. I have talked with atheists or agnostics who, during their lifetime, denied the existence of God or a "Higher Power." They quickly begin to doubt their unbelief when faced with their own inevitable and imminent death.

In the story "Afterlife," I will tell you about an unofficial study conducted on several patients in a coronary care unit. These patients had just experienced a cardiac arrest. These fortunate patients survived the near death experience though they hovered between life and death for a short period of time. The patients' answers to the survey questions were not surprising. With the exception of one man's account of his journey into Hell, the descriptions of the dying process were of a peaceful trip down a beautiful river. This same heavenly place is described in many of the books written about the near death experience.

One of the duties at my current job is to pronounce patients who have passed from this life into the next. Recently, I went into a room to pronounce a patient who had died. A family member stopped me and said, "What an awful job you have. I'd hate to have to do what you do every time someone dies."

His comment surprised me. I never thought of the job as morbid or demeaning. When I really stop to think about it, I feel that it is humbling to be the person who by declaring death has also announced the transition from this life into the next. Maybe it's because I believe that there is something far better that awaits each of us after our short existence on earth. Maybe it's because I see the cessation of pain and suffering on the face of the deceased. Whatever the reason, I don't see death as an ugly, dreaded monster that stalks people until it finally pounces and captures its victim. Death to me is a journey toward something far grander than what I've experienced in this life.

Looking death in the face is hard for many people. Sometimes it is the fear of the unknown.

Many patients experience dread and anxiety over the idea of excruciating pain. Many are afraid that they won't be able to say the things that are important to their loved ones. People who are dying are forced to deal with regrets. Things that may have been forgotten or buried for years will resurface with clarity when death knocks at the door.

The hardest thing about dying for most patients is saying goodbye. The dying patient can sense that the family or loved one is not ready for them to die. In many instances a patient will hang on for days and sometimes weeks. It is not until one certain loved one leans over and says, "It is okay to let go," that the patient will then relax, close his eyes and cease to breathe. It seems so natural and peaceful when a patient senses from his loved ones that it is okay to die.

Death is a sure thing for all of us, but it doesn't have to be faced with fear. It is but a stepping stone from this realm to the next. It is with hope that people can face their own death. Death does not have to cause us terror or dread. It can be encountered with peace and the anticipation of what comes next.

> *If in this life only we have hope in Christ, we are of all men most miserable* (1 Corinthians 15:19 KJV).

The Nurse

But ye, brethren, be not weary in well doing (2 Thessalonians 3:18 KJV).

As I made rounds in the Medical Intensive Care Unit (MICU), Shannon, the team leader, told me that the patient in room eight was going to arrest. The 61-year-old woman had been in the MICU on a ventilator for over a week. I walked into the room with Shannon and saw a morbidly obese woman lying in a comatose state. She was surrounded by machines, cables and lines. Despite her third unit of blood that evening, the woman's skin was the color of the sheet that covered her cold and lifeless body. The woman had no blood pressure. Her pulse was fast and she had an erratic heart rhythm. Despite the four drugs being pumped into her body, the woman was actively dying.

The patient's nurse, Pam, made telephone calls to the woman's primary care physician, surgeon, intensivist, brother and two sisters. Shannon stayed in the room with the patient and held onto the dying woman's hand for the next twenty minutes while the rest of the staff stood back waiting for the angel of death to enter the room. There was nothing anybody could do. The woman had been to surgery two times already. Her infection was systemic and massive. Her lab work was very abnormal and suggested multi-system failure. After talking to the woman's sister, Pam got the order for the patient to have a Do Not Resuscitate (DNR) status. We all stood in the room, watching as she slipped away.

The woman's sister asked Pam to call a priest. It was after 1 a.m. and there was not a clergy member in the hospital. I dialed the number of the priest who was on call but he didn't answer. Leaving a message on his machine, I told him the patient would not live much longer and that he was needed immediately. The priest did not arrive in time so the nurses in the room that night prayed for the dying woman.

I stepped out of the room for a few minutes to complete some paperwork. As I walked back into the room, I saw Shannon holding the woman's hand. She was touching her face and arm and telling the woman that it was okay to die. Shannon told the woman that her sister called and said, "I love you." She held onto the patient's hand and said, "You're not alone. We are here with you. It's okay to let go now." Minutes later, the woman died.

I thanked Shannon and Pam for staying with the patient. In fact all of the nurses in MICU that night came in and out of the room on frequent occasions. They were all there for the patient's death. The woman did not die alone. Shannon looked at me and said, "I can't let her die alone. No one should have to die without knowing that there is someone with them."

What happened that night defines nursing. Despite the sometimes rough exterior and the blunt and sometimes seemingly uncaring attitude of nurses, there is still the giving, loving and tender heart of the nurse who entered the profession to help ease the pain of illness and suffering in others.

Many times when a patient or family member calls me with a complaint about a nurse, I want to walk them into a room where a nurse like Shannon stands beside a dying patient and simply stays as the patient passes from this life into the next. I want these people not only to witness the true compassion and empathy of the nurse but also to see how hard it is to face death everyday . . . how it takes a little piece of the nurse's heart every time one of her patients dies.

Even though death is always waiting around the corner and the complaints are sometimes many, the nurse comes back to work day after day. Sometimes walls get built around hearts that have been touched by too much death, too much pain and too much loss. But I'm convinced that behind every wall is a tender, caring heart that desires to do whatever it takes to help ease the suffering of someone else.

After 30 years of nursing, I think that I can say with surety that nurses don't stay nurses because of a title or money or perks. Nurses are nurses because of what is in their hearts.

Shawn

…Or when saw we thee sick or in prison and came unto thee? And the King shall answer and say unto them, Verily I say unto you, Insasmuch as ye have done it unto one of the least of these my brethren, ye have done it unto me. (St. Matthew 25:39,40, KJV).

While standing in the checkout line at the grocery store today, I read this headline: "Senator offers 25 million dollars for a cure for his cancer." Death has a way of prioritizing life. This wealthy politician was willing to give away a large part of his fortune for a chance to live just a little longer. Death is humbling. Many will beg or bargain for just a few more days or weeks of life.

Reading the headlines about the dying senator caused me to think about Shawn. I met this dying, 55-year-old man a few months ago while working the night shift. I received a call a little after midnight. The nurse in charge asked me to come over to the unit. She said that they had a situation and they weren't sure how to handle it. When I arrived on the unit, I was directed to Shawn's room.

Shawn was dying of metastatic cancer of the liver. He had long, spindly arms and legs. He had a round and taut abdomen. He had developed the appearance of a long overdue pregnant woman. His abdomen was full of fluid that had accumulated there because of his nonfunctioning liver, the result of cancer. Shawn's color was grayish gold. His eyes were droopy and his expression said, "I'm tired of this. I've had enough."

When I first walked into his room, Shawn was attempting to sit straight up in the bed. He was trying to get comfortable. His days of lying down in the bed are over. There is so much fluid in his abdomen that if he reclines even slightly, the pressure on his lungs prevents expansion. Shawn is unable to breathe unless he sits up at a 90 degree angle.

When I introduced myself, Shawn's eyes met mine for a few brief seconds before he looked away. I took his hand in mine and looked at him until he again made eye contact with me. Sometimes there are no words to say when encountering the suffering patient who has reached the "end of life" stage. I could do nothing but look at this man who had obviously suffered much.

I had been called to come to assist the nurses in dealing with the fact that Shawn was caught trying to end his own life. He had gotten out of bed, taken a flower vase, broke it into jagged pieces and went to the far corner of the room. Shawn had a piece of glass in his hand and was found tearing at the flesh around his throat. He was attempting to connect the jagged piece of glass with one of the large blood vessels in his neck. There was a lot of blood and several long bleeding cuts on both sides of his neck. Because of his weakened state or perhaps it was the timing of the nurse's rounds, Shawn was found and was not able to effectively complete the task of ending his own life. Of more importance to Shawn was the fact that he was unable to stop the pain that he was forced to endure every moment of every day.

There were numerous, red and jagged cuts along both sides of Shawn's neck. By the time I reached his room, Shawn was back in bed with his neck cleaned of the blood. The glass shards were placed in a bag but for what reason I wasn't sure. Probably to be offered as proof of Shawn's terrible deed.

When I took Shawn's hand in my gloveless hand, one of the nurses whispered, "Be careful. He has hepatitis C." As my eyes met his, I failed to see anything but the pain and exhaustion of a dying man. As I stood holding his hand, Shawn looked at me and whispered, "I'm sorry! I didn't mean to cause anybody grief. I don't want to be a problem. I'm just tired of the pain. I can't stand it anymore."

Whether he expected a lecture or some type of reprimand for his actions, I wasn't sure. I was certain that it would not be from me or any of the nurses in the room that night. I asked Shawn, "What can we do to help you?"

Shrugging his thin shoulders, Shawn said, "There is nothing anyone can do."

Many times it is outside the realm of medical science or human ability to help those who are facing their own death. Science can provide medications for the pain and nausea and they do help some of the time. In Shawn's case, he was already on three narcotics that when given at the prescribed dose and time, gave him relief for a few minutes. What Shawn was looking for was escape or a reprieve . . . the kind that comes with permanent sleep.

"What do I say to help this man?" I asked God as I stood holding Shawn's hand. Surrounded by the nursing staff, most of whom had been RNs for only a short period of time, I made the decision to offer the only thing that I knew could help Shawn. I asked Shawn if he would like for me to pray for him. Grabbing both of my hands in his, he quickly and emphatically said, "Yes, please . . . right now!"

So while holding both of Shawn's hands in mine, I prayed for this dying man. It was hard to hold back the tears but I knew that Shawn needed to hear about the hope that comes from God. He needed to hear about the hope that exists even for the dying. I prayed asking God for relief from the pain and suffering. I asked for complete healing according to His will, and if this was not to be then I asked for strength to endure.

When I opened my eyes and looked at Shawn, he had tears in his eyes. He also had a peaceful expression on his face. He smiled and thanked me for caring enough to pray for him.

Looking around at the nursing staff, I was a bit surprised to see that everyone had stepped out of the room. When I peered around the curtain, they were all standing outside the door. Some had tears in their eyes. No one seemed to know what to say. Shawn died the following morning.

God tells us to live by example. As a nurse of 30 years, I've seen much of what sickness and death can do to people, not only to the patient but also to the nurses who deal with the dying everyday. I want those nurses to see that it is possible to hold onto the ability to have compassion for the dying patient regardless of his past or his diagnosis. It is possible to offer care to those who depend on us without judging them. When science and the health care team have no more answers, I hope that they will realize the importance of someone being there to pray with the patient. I hope these nurses will be willing to hold a hand, look into desperate eyes and say, "I can't do anything more for you but I know someone who can. I'm here and I'll pray with you."

Liaison

The last enemy that shall be destroyed is death (1 Corinthians 15:26 KJV).

It was the Christmas holiday. The entire pediatric cardiology clinic was empty for the Christmas weekend. It was a Friday afternoon, the 23rd of December. I had chosen to work that day because I was saving my vacation for maternity leave. I wanted as much time off as I could accumulate. There were a few of the pediatric cardiologists running around finishing up last minute details before the long Christmas weekend. But other than two or three physicians, a pediatric cardiology fellow and myself, there was no one else in the department.

The pediatric cardiology clinic at Texas Children's Hospital specializes in the care of children with congenital or acquired heart disease as well as cardiac arrhythmias. The clinic is normally busy from 7 a.m. to 7 p.m., Monday through Friday. Pat, one of the other RNs in the clinic, and I worked in the subspecialty department of pediatric cardiology electrophysiology. My job was that of monitoring and educating children and their parents about slow heart rates, pacemakers and the electrophysiology study done to diagnose the conduction disorder. Pat was responsible for monitoring and educating children and parents about fast cardiac rhythms, medications to control the rhythm and the electrophysiology study done to diagnose the exact cause of the tachyarrhythmia (fast rhythm). There were three pediatric cardiology electro-physiologists, two RNs, and sometimes three or four pediatric cardiology fellows who would spend a year or two learning the subspecialty of pediatric electrophysiology. I coordinated the pacemaker clinic and Pat ran the arrhythmia clinic. Our jobs were often interchangeable, and we frequently covered for one another.

There were two other nurses in the pediatric cardiology department. Sue and Mary Ann's jobs were to act as liaisons between the pediatric cardiologist, the patient's family and the pediatric cardiology surgeons, as well as the children. Sue and Mary Ann spent much of their day traveling between the catheterization (cath) lab, the operating room, the pediatric intensive care unit (PICU) and the open-heart recovery room, delivering news about a child who had undergone cardiac catheterization or open heart surgery. One of the two nurses would be assigned to a child and family. That nurse would then provide pre-cath or pre-op teaching as well as teaching and support during the child's hospitalization and care. On the day of the procedure, Sue or Mary Ann would make at least hourly trips from the cath lab or the operating room to the waiting room, delivering news and updates to the anxious parents, grandparents, siblings and various other family members.

Most of the children who came to the clinic had been born with severe debilitating heart anomalies that required repeat cardiac catheterizations and open-heart surgeries. A large majority of these children never lived past the age of 20, despite the radical heart procedures performed on them. Many of the children developed a fatal heart rhythm, infection, heart failure or other post-operative complication that halted life at an early age. The children came from various areas of the United States and many other countries.

Pat and I quickly fell in love with most of the children who came in and out of the pediatric cardiology clinic. We didn't directly care for all of them, but a large percentage of the kids developed some type of arrhythmia eventually as a result of their heart surgery. Because the clinic was a small, specialized group, everyone knew each other.

On this particular Friday afternoon before Christmas, I received a call from one of the pediatric cardiologists. He asked me to go to the Emergency Department (ED) and "check" a patient there. Thinking that I would be checking a child's pacemaker, I loaded up my machine and made my way to the ED. Pat was off for the long weekend. I had not seen Sue or Mary Ann but assumed that they would be on call for their area of the clinic. What I didn't know was that I had been given the job of covering for everybody since I was the only RN working that Friday.

After asking the doctor why he didn't have the patient brought up to the clinic instead of being checked in the ED, he shrugged his shoulders, mumbled some unintelligible words, and walked away.

As I approached the ED nurse's station, several of the nurses stared at me as I pushed my pacemaker equipment ahead of me. Pointing to a closed door, one of the nurses murmured, "She's in there."

I should have thought the situation through before pushing into the room, but I assumed that I would be going in to do the job of checking and reprogramming a child's pacemaker. As I barged into the room, I saw a young mother and father holding onto each other. They were crying and attempting to comfort one another. Across the room was a little woman who sat in the corner quietly weeping.

My eyes were finally drawn to a small child lying on a stretcher in the center of the room. The child was as white as the sheet that covered her tiny body. There was an endotrachial (breathing) tube protruding from her mouth. Intravenous bags hung on both sides of her body. The parents would walk over to their dead child, stroke her arm, kiss her face and then break out sobbing. I stood frozen in the doorway with my pacemaker equipment. Looking back and forth from the parents to the grandmother to the child, I could only stand there and stare.

"Why did she have to die now? Couldn't God have allowed us to have her for Christmas?" asked the mother. "She was so excited about the tree and Santa Claus. What will we do with all her gifts? She made it through the surgery and did so well."

"Why did this happen now?" asked the father.

The parents continued to ask questions to no one in particular. Who would have the answers to their questions anyway? Certainly, I had no answers for them. I was still stuck in the doorway unsure of what to do. I knew that I couldn't walk out and leave. But I also knew that I would not be of much comfort to any of them. I had never had to deal with the death of a child. I'd had seen several adult patients die in my seven years as a nurse, but never had I dealt with a young child's death.

The pediatric cardiologist came in then and looked at me with a pleading look in his eyes. He asked, "Can you take care of them?" Numbly or maybe dumbly, I nodded my head. I noticed then that he had been crying. He walked over to the parents and awkwardly put his hand on their shoulders. He then broke down in tears and walked out of the room.

By this time, I had adjusted to the situation, but I remained standing just inside the door. I wanted nothing more than to run out of the room just as the doctor had done. I wanted to run out and yell at the nurses who failed to let me in on the situation. Knowing that I couldn't leave, I remained inside the room. The physician was depending on me to be the liaison that Friday afternoon.

Being four months pregnant did not help my already unstable emotional condition. After what seemed like an hour, I finally moved toward the parents who were now bent over their 18-month-old child. They were talking to each other about the good times they had experienced with their little girl. The grandmother saw me crying and, for lack of a better description, "losing it." She came over and put her arms around me and actually tried to comfort me. I looked at her and said, "I'm sorry. I should be giving you comfort." She smiled and hugged me as we both cried for the family's loss.

When I look back on that Friday over 20 years ago, the details are still exact in my memory. I believe it was the hardest death that I've had to be involved with. My respect level for Sue and Mary Ann rose immensely that day, and I believe that people who do a job like theirs are God's angels on earth.

The loss of a child is the most painful thing that can be experienced in life. As many times as I've seen it happen since that Friday afternoon 20 years ago, I still have a hard time dealing with it. I pray to God that I never have to go through that kind of pain. For those who have may God, who experienced the death of His only Son, give you peace and strength to endure.

Suicide

And the peace of God which passeth all understanding shall keep your hearts and minds through Christ Jesus (Philippians 4:7 KJV).

Lanna was the 22-year-old mother of a two-year-old girl. She had been in and out of various hospital psychiatric units from the time she was a pre-teenager. Lanna's parents loved her despite her many problems with alcohol and drug addictions. She had been plagued with addictions and mental illness for most of her life.

On a Friday night in July around 9 p.m., Lanna got into an argument with her boyfriend. They were at his house, and she grabbed his 22-gauge pistol. After asking him if he dared her to pull the trigger, she put the gun into her mouth and shot herself. Lanna died instantly.

Lanna's boyfriend scooped her 90 pound frame into his arms, placed her in his truck and drove the short five minute trip to the ER. As he burst through the ER doors, he shouted, "Help me! She shot herself!"

Lanna was pronounced dead on arrival. An attempt was made to resuscitate her, but to no avail. A skull x-ray was done immediately and showed that the bullet had traveled through the roof of her mouth and a mass of brain tissue. It was lodged between brain tissue and the skull. Along the path of the bullet was evidence of the hemorrhage caused by the shell. There was nothing anyone could do for Lanna. She was gone.

Lanna's parents were called to the hospital. The ER physician, the nurse in charge of the ER that night and I went into the family room right after they arrived. As nursing supervisor, one of my duties was to be present when a family was told of the death of their loved one. Lanna's parents sat quietly while the doctor explained that she died instantly and had suffered no pain.

There were no tears as Lanna's mother looked around the room and said, "She is finally at peace. She has been troubled for so many years. Now she'll be able to rest from all of her problems."

Here was a couple who had just lost their only daughter to suicide. It was a senseless and selfish act of desperation. Lanna left behind a two-year-old who would now be entrusted to the care of these two people, her grandparents. This two-year-old would never know her own mother. She would probably have no memory of the two years they had spent together. Looking at Lanna's parents, I wondered what they had lived through with their daughter to believe that she would finally be at peace and better off in death.

Nobody said anything for a few long seconds, so I looked at Lanna's dad and asked, "Do you want me to call a minister or a priest?"

"What do we need someone like that for?" he shouted at me as he rose to his feet and came to stand over me.

His face was purple with rage and the blood vessels in his neck were bulging. I seriously thought that he wanted to strike me for asking the question. I have witnessed many people deal with the death of a loved one by expressing anger, but I was really afraid that this man was going to lose control and hit me.

I wished that I could offer him words of comfort and encouragement. I wanted to tell him about peace that passes all understanding even at this difficult time in his life. But he didn't want to hear it.

It seemed that this grieving couple had a warped belief system. Yes, they were angry at God because of their daughter's untimely death. They believed that Lanna was now at rest in Heaven. They didn't want to acknowledge that there was a God who could offer them peace and comfort at this time, even though they believed that their daughter was now in a heavenly realm with Him.

Suicide is not an easy subject to talk about. In fact, it is not politically correct to label the killing of one's self suicide. In most cases it is defined as a symptom of severe mental illness or depression. It is listed as a side effect of some anti-anxiety or psychotropic medications. The literature says suicide is not the fault of the person who takes his own life. It is the fault of society and life's pressures.

While a student in nursing school, I lived in a city that had an overwhelming drug problem. Many of the young men and women of the town were grandchildren or great grandchildren of wealthy oil tycoons. During the late 1950s, there was no longer an oil boom in the town. The wealthy people were long gone, leaving behind a generation of children (pre-Baby Boomers) who lived off the wealth of their parents. They didn't have to go to college or prepare to earn a living. This wealth eventually dried up, as did the extravagant living and spending of many people in the town. This generation had bred a new generation of children who still had the family name but none of the wealth. There were few jobs in the city and a very poor work ethic. There was a lot of poverty as well as a large population of drug or alcohol addicted people.

A close friend in college was a resident of the city, and she introduced me to various family members and friends. One evening, we went to a party hosted by a couple of nursing students in our class. Also attending the party that night were some young men who were, as my friend called them, suicide cultists. She told a story that made me shudder.

In her local high school, there was a group of 14 boys who got together one night and made a pact among themselves. They promised each other that they would all commit suicide sometime prior to or following graduation from high school. These boys had no ambition for college, technical school or a job. They had no desire for a wife and family. They had promised each other that they would end their life together at a young age.

On the night of the party, I met four of the young men. They were the only four left. The other ten had gone through with their promise to commit suicide. I was shocked and morbidly mesmerized by these four boys who laughed and talked with everyone as though their lives were normal. I stood back and listened as the conversation eventually came around to the subject of their suicide pact. One boy expressed regret over making the commitment to the other 13 boys.

He was asked, "Why don't you just walk away?"

He replied, "I can't let the others down . . . can't let them die alone. They're waiting for me."

The other three boys were surrounded by a large crowd and soaked up the attention. Wherever they went, the suicide pact was talked about. They were heroes or celebrities. It was one of the most disturbing scenes I had ever witnessed.

As I listened to the boys talk about death and suicide, I asked God these questions: Didn't any of them ever go to church and hear about Jesus Christ? Didn't they know that suicide was a selfish and senseless act that hurt not only themselves but their family and friends? How did they get so caught up in Satan's scheme?

Leaving the party that night, I thought about the hopelessness of these boys. What must their lives have been like to want to end them just as they were starting? I thanked God that I had a relationship with Him and that no matter how bad things seemed, I was never alone. He was always there for me.

One day, fourteen years later, I was working as a home health nurse in the same town. As I made my last visit for the day, I entered the home of an elderly couple. Before I could get my coat off, the woman asked if she could show me something. I noticed that her husband rolled his eyes as he said her name in exasperation. She ignored him and began walking out of the room, leading me down a flight of steps. She opened the door at the bottom of the stairs, and inside was a shrine. There were candles along the walls and in the front of the room. There was an altar of sorts along one wall, and placed on it were more candles, crosses, and several statues of the Virgin Mary. Among all of these religious artifacts were pictures of a blond-haired boy of about 19 or 20 years of age. They were pictures of her only son, Alex.

"He died 14 years ago," she said. "He had a misfortunate accident. He fell from the bridge and died."

After offering condolences, I backed out of the room. It was a very bizarre scene. Here was a 70-year-old woman who had built a shrine to her deceased son, her only child. It had been in her home for nearly 15 years.

When I finished my visit, I went back to the office. The unhealthy ritual of this woman was discussed. I had made this home health visit for another nurse in the office who couldn't get there that day. She told me that the mother got up at 6 a.m. every day to light candles and pray for Alex. She then went down several times during the day, sometimes for hours at a time. At night, she and her husband would go down to the shrine to pray and tell their son goodnight.

The whole story was very unusual and unhealthy. What stunned me were the comments made by the woman's regular nurse. She said, "Alex belonged to a group of boys who had made a suicide pact back in the late 1970s. He was one of the last of the group of boys to die. He jumped off the bridge after using LSD. He had a drug addiction. His mom cannot accept the fact that he killed himself, so she prays for his soul several hours a day."

As I perform my duties as a nursing supervisor, I hear of the suicide attempts and deaths that come into the ER. They are frequent. The death certificates no longer label the demise suicide. It is not politically correct to do so. With a suicide, there are feelings of hopelessness for the family and friends as well as the health care workers. There is never closure for the loved ones of the person who dies by their own hand.

A few years ago, my father's 92-year-old friend decided that he could not tolerate the pain and isolation of life. He made the decision to end it all with his revolver and a self inflicted gun-shot wound to the head. He had lived for 92 years and death couldn't come fast enough for him.

Life for many people in society today has become so painful that they want it to end. People are seeking an escape from the pressures of life. Many use alcohol or drugs. Some desperate souls resort to suicide. But how does that affect those who are left to deal with the violent death?

Lanna's mom said, "She just wanted peace." That is the desire of so many people in this world today. They need to know that there is a peace, and it doesn't have to be temporary. It doesn't leave when the alcohol or drug wears off. Suicide will not bring this peace. The peace I refer to is a permanent peace, and it will sustain a person through all of life's ups and downs. This peace is found in a relationship with Jesus Christ.

These things I have spoken unto you, that in me ye might have peace. In the world ye shall have tribulation: but be of good cheer; I have overcome the world (John 16:33 KJV).

Choices

Behold, I shew you a mystery; We shall not all sleep, but we shall all be changed, In a moment, in the twinkling of an eye, at the last trump: for the trumpet shall sound, and the dead shall be raised incorruptible, and we shall be changed. For this corruptible must put on incorruption, and this mortal must put on immortality. So when this corruptible shall have put on incorruption, and this mortal shall have put on immortality, then shall be brought to pass the saying that is written, Death is swallowed up in victory. O death, where is thy sting? O grave, where is thy victory? (1 Corinthians 15:51–55 KJV).

The call came one Wednesday morning in February. My husband, Kelley, had just received the following message from his sister: "Mom is being sent home from the hospital to die. She refuses a feeding tube. She can't eat or drink anything without it going into her lungs, and there is nothing else they can do if she refuses a feeding tube."

We were not sure of a time frame, but we knew that we needed to leave as soon as possible. Kelley and I took a leave from our jobs, packed up the car, and left for Florida that same Wednesday evening. Lexie and Blake, our two older children, had just finished midterms and made the decision to go with us. They were able to get away for about a week and wanted to be there with their grandmother. Our youngest daughter, Taylor, who was 12, stayed at home with her grandparents. We realized that we would be watching Kelley's mom, Norma, slowly pass out of this life. It was not something for a child to have to watch.

As we arrived at Norma's house, there were many emotions that we experienced. These emotions included the fear of death so close and imminent, shame over not keeping in contact as much as we should have, anger at seeing Norma spend her last year of life debilitated and confined to a wheelchair, and worry that her own three children would never again see her art and the family heirlooms that had been collected and passed down through the years.

When Kelley entered her room, Norma attempted to pull herself up in the bed. She smiled from ear to ear and kept touching his face. Kelley had not seen his mom in nearly two years. He was just glad to have been given the chance to spend the last seven days of her life sitting by her side.

Norma had hospice nurses who came in to check on her every day. She wasn't able to swallow any food or liquid, including water. The hospice nurses explained that we could wet her mouth with pink sponges on a stick, so this was done frequently throughout the day. Norma had been ordered Ativan and Morphine to help ease the process of dying. She would have nothing to do with any of the medications. She was leaving this world with her thinking and memory as intact as possible. Every time the medications were offered, she would adamantly shake her head, "No."

We sat with Norma day after day for a week, watching her get weaker and thinner. She was unable to communicate her needs because of her nonfunctioning throat muscles. This was the result of a stroke several years before. She could say one or two words occasionally, and for the most part, she understood what we said to her. But toward the fourth and fifth day, she seemed to fade in and out of reality.

During the periods of alertness, Lexie and Blake took turns reading to Norma from a book her son, Kevin, had brought. The book, *The Five People You Meet in Heaven* by Mitch Albom, seemed to be God-sent. Norma would raise her eyebrows and smile at appropriate times during the reading of the book. If Lexie or Blake wasn't in the room, other family members or some of her close friends would pick up the book and begin reading. Norma was a Christian and believed in a life after this one. She was ready to die and had no fear of what came next.

As an artist, Norma had a very vivid imagination. She always thought and acted so many years younger than her stated age. She was very wise and had a variety of life experiences, which she frequently put on canvas until the stroke took that ability away from her. Because of her personality, this particular book seemed so fitting for Norma. We talked about who would be the five people she might meet in heaven. Of course, she couldn't say much, but with her eyes and her smile or frown we were able to figure out who she couldn't wait to see once she passed from this life to the next.

Norma had touched so many people's lives during her short 74 years on earth. Her sister, Marilyn, and she were very much alike. When I first saw them together, I thought that they were twins. They both loved arts and crafts, antiques, camping, fishing and clean cars. They talked alike, and both had that calm, "whatever will be, will be" attitude about life.

Norma had seen tragedy in her life. She had lost her husband at 47 years of age. Her oldest son died at 43 years of age. Because of her loss and determination she was able to take over the family insurance business and run it successfully until the day she sold it. She had developed a strength that is missing in most women. This strength allowed Norma to courageously look her own imminent death in the face and say, "Go ahead. I'm not afraid."

During the last two years of my job as an ICU nurse, I questioned much of what health care professionals do in order to keep a patient alive. Many elderly people are capable of making their own decisions about long-term ventilator care and/or the placement of a feeding tube in order to prolong life. If the patient is able to say, "No" or "Stop," the staff refers to the family member to make the decision for the patient. If the family is left to make the decision, then more times than not, the patient's decision to come off the ventilator or refuse the feeding tube is ignored.

I left the ICU setting because I felt that the wishes of patients are overlooked. If a patient decides to have a ventilator removed, stop dialysis or refuse the placement of a feeding tube, this patient is deemed incompetent. It seems that the health care profession infringes on the patient's right to choose. Many of the patients who are ventilator-dependent require a feeding tube. In the many years I cared for this type of patient, I've seen only one or two go home. The majority are sent to long-term ventilator units or nursing homes that manage ventilator patients. Many of the patients are alert, oriented and able to make their own decisions about their future, but many times the health care staff refers to the family to make the decisions. I have seen instances where a psychiatrist was called in to declare the patient mentally incompetent and therefore incapable of making their own decisions, just because the patient chose to die rather than live their life dependent on a ventilator and feeding tube.

When Norma made the choice to refuse the feeding tube and the doctors and family honored her wishes, I applauded them. There is very little that is as depressing as an elderly person who is placed in a total care environment (nursing home) away from their home, their belongings, their pets and their family. Some people choose that type of life when they become dependent on others for their care, and that is okay if it is what the patient wants. It was not Norma's choice. She chose death and the life after this one rather than a feeding tube and total dependency on others for her life.

At day five, Norma was wide awake. She had not slept in more than 48 hours. Even though she faded in and out of a stuperous state, she refused medications either for pain or to help her sleep. Her sons and daughter, as well as the rest of her family, stayed constantly at her side. Jodi, Kevin, and Kelley would lie beside her during the night and sleep short periods of time. She didn't sleep much, especially toward the end. I don't know if she was afraid to close her eyes, but when her children would tell her to close her eyes and rest for awhile, she'd just smile. Norma finally went to sleep around 2 p.m. on February 22 and passed away around 10 a.m. on the morning of February 23, 2006.

During my years as an ICU nurse, I have witnessed many deaths. I have never seen anybody die with such peace as Norma did that morning in February. The sun was shining and the sky was blue. The air was warm, and the birds continued to sing. Norma's artistic touch from the flowers to the décor of her house continued on even though she moved from this life to the next. What a brave lady she was right up to the end. I saw the determination in her eyes. She never exhibited fear or regret. She just lived life to the end.

If in this life only we have hope in Christ, we are of all men most miserable (1 Corinthians 15:19 KJV).

Friend

For he shall give his angels charge over thee, to keep thee in all thy ways (Psalm 91:11 KJV).

While working in the ICU, I was occasionally assigned to the code team. When a Cardiac Arrest Team (CAT) was called, the nurses assigned would be required to report to the place of the arrest and intervene during a cardiac or respiratory emergency.

A CAT is called when a patient is found with a life-threatening arrhythmia, has no pulse, has stopped breathing or is having severe metabolic or respiratory distress.

One of my assigned duties one particular evening was to respond as part of the arrest team. During an arrest, a number of people attend to the patient, including one or two ICU nurses, an ED physician, one or two respiratory therapists, an anesthesia team member, a member of the IV team, an ECG technician, the nursing supervisor, the patient's nurse and the team leader for the unit where the patient is assigned. There are normally more nurses present. They are the ones who get the patient into bed, get the arrest board under the patient, bring the crash cart to the bedside, begin CPR if indicated and rescue breathe for the patient. It is the MICU nurse assigned to arrests to be the code team leader until the ED physician arrives.

It was a Monday evening in July of 2001. My friend, Kay, had just had a stress test, a heart catheterization and subsequent quadruple-bypass surgery. Kay had experienced chest and jaw pain a few days before this and was found to have four coronary artery blockages. She underwent Coronary Artery Bypass Grafting (CABG) on the 26th of July. By the 29th she had done so well that she was transferred out of the Surgical Intensive Care Unit (SICU) to the telemetry, or step-down, unit of the hospital.

Before I went on my dinner break that evening, I stopped over to visit Kay. She looked good but wasn't quite back to her normal, smiling self. Kay had done remarkably well during and after the surgery but she didn't feel as well as she had earlier in the day. She gave me a half-hearted smile as I said goodbye, telling her that I'd pray for her. As I walked back to my unit, I did just that. Saying a quick prayer for her complete recovery and cessation of pain, I went back to work.

I had not been back in my unit for ten minutes when the cardiac arrest team was called to the step-down unit, room 6113W. My heart sank as I ran out the door to the arrest. Knowing that I was running to Kay's room, I asked one of the other nurses to go with me. As I ran down the hall to Kay's room, I saw her husband, Bob and two of her very good friends anxiously standing in the hall.

Arriving in the room, I saw one of the SICU nurses directing the code. Thankfully, I was positioned at Kay's head where I took her hand and whispered prayers in her ear. Normally, I would have been responsible to hook up the monitor and administer the defibrillating shock to the heart or direct the team in medications according to rhythm until the ED physician arrived. I believe that God prevented me from having to do this because not only did one of my co-workers come with me to the arrest, but one of the SICU nurses happened to be there that evening. I believe that I would have had a hard time working as part of the arrest team on a lady who had been a friend of mine for more than 20 years.

Kay and I played music together at conventions and church events from the time I was a teenager. It was Kay who taught me at a young age that friendship has no age barrier. Kay is about 14 years older than I. She and I went to the same events and she would always ask, "Do you want to play organ or piano?" I nearly always played piano, but since I knew that she would rather not have to be stuck on the organ every time, once in a while we would trade spots. We used to sit at the front of the church or auditorium and watch the crowd, pointing out things of interest to each other. Many times we laughed at what we saw even though we were at a church function.

Hanging out with Kay was like hanging out with one of my teen friends. Over the years we stopped playing music together, but when her son married my sister our friendship became cemented for the duration.

When I walked into that room the night of her cardiac arrest, it was as if a space around the bed opened up for me at her left side. I took her hand immediately after she had been shocked out of a lethal rhythm. She was jolted into a subconscious state, and her first words as she opened her eyes were, "Jesus, help me!" I stayed beside her and talked to her as the team stabilized her rhythm and got her ready for transport back to the SICU.

Kay and I have crossed paths on a sporadic basis at the hospital since that night. It seems that her hospital admissions are during my shift or to the unit where I work. I believe that God places each one of us where He can use us. Kay's son, Bob, refers to these times as divine appointments.

We all could sit back and look at certain coincidences in life when we've been at the right place at the right time. Those divine appointments place us in a position where we can be God's angels on earth. He has called us to help others. We are to be a friend and neighbor to those in need. It makes life easier to know that we are not alone—that there are people everywhere who care about what happens to us. Those angels or people who have a divine appointment with us will be right there where God has positioned them.

Humility

But he giveth more grace. Wherefore he saith, God resisteth the proud, but giveth grace unto the humble (James 4:6 KJV).

Certain events in life can humble us at the most unexpected moments. My church sent a team of youth to perform at a church in Ashland, KY one weekend in July. We traveled for seven hours one Friday evening in order to perform at the Saturday night concert. The entire drama team could not go because of the distance, but there were approximately 15 team members and three adults who made the trek. The drama team performed dance routines, mimed, signed and acted to contemporary Christian music. The team was scheduled to perform twice that evening.

The church was packed with an enthusiastic, fun crowd of youths as well as young and older adults. What happened that Saturday night changed forever the views and attitudes of the entire drama team. That night, we witnessed true worship.

The performers that evening sang, played various instruments, danced and acted out skits centering on various moral and biblical issues. As the night was coming to a close, the youth director of the church announced a solo to be sung by Tim, a 15-year-old boy from the host church. As we watched, the young man slowly and awkwardly lumbered up onto the stage. It was obvious that Tim suffered from some sort of debilitating neuromuscular disease.

Tim stood on the stage smiling from ear to ear. He was so glad to be given a chance to perform his talent in front of such a large audience. The song that Tim chose to sing was an old hymn that everyone knew. As he started to sing, his voice quivering, I realized that had I not been familiar with the song, not one word of the lyrics would have been understandable. As Tim sang all four verses of "Amazing Grace," I looked around the audience at the people seated in the pews. There was not a noise in the place. Tears streamed down the faces of most of the young people and adults as Tim mesmerized the crowd with his performance. The song was sung with honest sincerity of the heart. The notes were wrong much of the time, the song was off key and the words were unintelligible, but it was sung from the heart.

At the beginning of the song, I was embarrassed for Tim, thinking, "How does he have the courage to stand in front of so many people and sing a song that no one can understand?" But as Tim kept singing, the song became beautiful. It was not because he sang in tune or pronounced the words so well, but because he made it true worship. He sang from his heart.

I learned humility, true humility, that night. The feeling can be conjured up every time I see or hear a person with cerebral palsy or muscular dystrophy. Most of us have so much to be thankful for and we take it for granted most of the time. Never will I forget that feeling of true humility that God allowed me the opportunity to witness. Humility is the one attribute that He requires of us all.

Afterlife

For the hope which is laid up for you in heaven, whereof ye heard before in the word of the truth of the gospel (Colossians 1:5 KJV).

Over the years, I have had many people ask me if I have ever seen anyone brought back from death. Because of my duties as an ICU nurse, I have seen and participated in many cardiac arrests. In many of the instances, the arrest team was able to get the fibrillating or non-beating heart to pump blood again or the once non-breathing patient to take a breath. Because of CPR and rescue breathing as well as current emergency drugs and medical procedures, people who cease to breathe or have a cardiac arrest (the stopping of the heart) don't have to die. In the hospital setting, I have seen many people live because of CPR and rescue breathing.

As a nurse in a 13-bed Coronary Care Unit in a large hospital in Houston, Texas, I witnessed and participated in cardiac arrests on a daily basis. There were days when I would attend a "code blue" or cardiac arrest three times in an eight-hour shift. Because of the nature of the hospital and unit, many patients were flown in from outlying hospitals throughout the state. Many of the patients were extremely sick with severe heart disease, so to witness and participate in a cardiac arrest or death was a normal part of any day.

As a child and teenager, I had an interest in afterlife experiences. I read a lot of books on the subject. The book may have included information about heaven and the afterlife, or it may have talked about ghosts and the supernatural. Whatever the perspective of the author, I would read the book.

Because I saw so many people experience death at my job, even if for only a few seconds or minutes, I became interested in hearing what the survivor had to say about the experience. These near-death experiences may have lasted for only a few seconds before the patient was shocked, paced or compressed back into a life-sustaining rhythm. Regardless of the time that the patient was "gone," I would make it a point to talk to the patient while taking an unofficial survey of the event.

Having talked with approximately 30 patients over an 18 month period, I found out information that coincided with what I had read as a youth. I asked questions such as, "What did you see? What did you feel? Were you in pain? Were you able to see what happened during the cardiac arrest? Where did you go?"

The answers of 29 of the patients were similar to the ones I had read about. The patients said that they felt no pain, only a sense of extreme peace. Some of the patients said that they were floating down a wide, beautiful river in a large garden. There were family and friends who had died years before, standing along the river banks with their hands outstretched. Everyone was smiling and excitedly awaiting their arrival. Some of the patients said they were walking through a cylinder-like tunnel toward a bright, white light. They felt peace and an anticipation to reach the light.

One of the patients described hovering above his hospital bed near the ceiling. He said that he saw the arrest team performing CPR. He saw the doctor placing a breathing tube, and he heard the conversation of the nurses and doctors. He said that he felt nothing and that he had no desire to return. In fact he felt no pain until he was resuscitated back to his mortal body.

The one and only patient that described the death experience as one of horror cried and wrung his hands as he described the event. He was hardly able to talk because of fear. This man said that he felt as though he were falling down a pitch-black hole. He fell in silence for a long period of time, and then he began to hear muffled screams. The man told me that the screams became louder and the air hotter, and then he was suddenly awake in his hospital bed.

The man asked me what had happened to him. I explained that he had suffered a cardiac arrest and that he had been shocked back to a normal heart rhythm. The man knew about heaven and hell and that what he had just described was not a description of heaven. That experience caused this man to pray and ask God for the forgiveness of sins. Right there in that hospital room, this man asked for another chance to live the life that God desired him to live.

After hearing the testimonials of these people who experienced cardiac arrest or a near-death experience, I am certain that there is life after death. There is a consequence for a life of sin and evil. The testimonials of the 30 people that I talked to are motivation for me to do whatever I can do to help others prepare for the eternal. I have a feeling that the one patient who experienced the fear, the fall, the heat and the screams during his cardiac arrest, now tells as many people as he can that there is a hell. It is not a place where people will get together and party with their friends. It is a place of pain and torment as Scripture describes it to be.

> *Correction is grievous unto him that forsaketh the way; and he that hateth reproof shall die. Hell and destruction are before the Lord: how much more then the hearts of the children of men?* (Proverbs 15:10, 11 KJV).

Death's Sting

*If in this life only we have hope in Christ, we are of all men most miserable (*1Corinthians 15:19 KJV*).*

As I walked into the office, the secretary told me that there had been a two-fatality accident on Route 38 North. As the blood began to drain from my face to my feet, she quickly added, "Your son called. He and your daughter are on their way home from school." Seeing my obvious anxiety and fear, she said, "They are okay!"

It was 5:30 p.m. on a Friday evening, and the roads were treacherous with ice and snow. I had just come from the ED where the staff was trying to prevent a Code Blue, or mass casualty situation. There were so many patients in the ED, the halls and the waiting area that there was no place to put another body. Several accidents in the area had just started arriving by ambulance. All I heard while in the ED was ambulance personnel reporting on horrible road conditions with accidents everywhere. It was nerve-wracking. I was already worried about my children, who were driving home from college. They had a 90 mile trip. Lexie and Blake left the campus around 4 p.m., and that would put them close to Route 38 North at around 5:30 p.m., the time of the fatal accident.

Becky had already told me that my son had called and said that they were okay but I couldn't ease my anxiety until I talked with either my son or daughter personally. When I sat down at the desk, I immediately dialed Blake's cell phone. He picked up on the second ring and assured me that he and his sister were alright. After hanging up with Blake, my anxiety eased, but then I started worrying about my sister, Bonnie. She was to leave her job in Butler around 6 p.m. and would be driving north on Route 38 to get home. I started thinking, "What if she left early and it was her that wrecked?" Remembering that there were two people in the car, I thought, "Maybe her husband rode home with her." My anxiety level again rose until I called the ambulance base to see if she had left yet. She was out on a call and was not anywhere near Route 38 North.

When I set my mind at ease about my two kids and my sister, I began thinking about all the people that I knew who would be driving north on Route 38 at that hour of the day. Isn't it amazing how worry and anxiety just plague us with questions like, "What if . . .?" "Could it be . . .?" "Do you think . . .?"

I thought about how I prayed during those ten minutes of worry and phone calls. I said things like, "Lord, please don't let it be my kids. And please don't let it be my sister or anybody in my family or my friends. And Lord, please don't let it be anyone from work. Or anyone I know or anyone related to people that I know."

My prayers were selfish. It was someone's family and loved ones who had died, and all I prayed for was that the deaths would not affect me in any manner. I wondered if my prayers were typical. I guess it is normal for us as humans to pray for less pain, less trouble, less tragedy and fewer problems from life.

For the rest of my shift, I could not stop thinking about the two unfortunate victims of the car accident. It was not until later that night that the names of the two victims were released. The tragic deaths were that of a mother and daughter. Both had been employees of the hospital a few years ago and were known by many of my co-workers. Their car had spun out of control on the icy roads and had broadsided an oncoming car. Both women were reportedly killed instantly from the impact of the accident. Both women left behind family members.

Life seems to deal cruel blows to people. Some seem to be affected more often than others with tragic events in life. Some seem to never feel the pain of a catastrophic loss. But it is just a matter of time before everyone will be touched by death or tragedy.

Guiltily, I drove home from work that night. I was thinking of how I had prayed that the deaths would not affect me. I had witnessed three deaths during my shift that evening. I was told of several more. I thought about all of the people who were touched by the pain and loss of death.

That evening alone, I attended the cardiac arrest and death of an 82-year-old man. I was given verbal reports of the death of two 40-year-old women. They both had passed away earlier that day with terminal cancer. During my shift that evening I was paged to go to another respiratory arrest and near death of a man with terminal lung problems. While at this arrest, a nursing friend told me that her 55-year-old father had been diagnosed with terminal lung cancer. He was given less than six months to live. It was overwhelming to hear about all of the death and pain around me that evening. As I made my way home that night, helpless feelings pervaded my spirit.

"What gives me the right to live accident or tragedy-free? What keeps me from having to stare death in the face or deal with the loss of a close family member? Not that I want to see tragedy or death, but I know that it's just around the corner waiting to pounce." I pondered these questions and thoughts on my drive home that night.

Praying for peace of mind, I asked God to relieve the anxiety and hopeless feelings. It is not for us to know why some people live and why some die.

I don't understand why some, especially the innocent, have to suffer tragic loss. I thank God every day for sheltering me from this pain and loss, but I have to admit that after nights like this, I worry when my turn will come. When will I have to deal with a tragedy or death of one of my family members?

As I drove I prayed for the families of the mother and daughter who were killed. I cried for the ten-year-old girl who had just lost her mother and grandmother. I also prayed for forgiveness for my selfish prayers that evening. But as I prayed for forgiveness, I knew in my heart that I would pray the same prayer the next time tragedy struck so close.

Is it wrong to want to avoid the pain and anxiety of loss in this life? I don't think so. But as Christians, we are to remember what Christ has to say about death. He tells us not to fear and that if we are His children, we should not be anxious about death.

Behold, I shew you a mystery; We shall not all sleep, but we shall all be changed, In a moment, in the twinkling of an eye, at the last trump: for the trumpet shall sound, and the dead shall be raised incorruptible, and we shall be changed. For this corruptible must put on incorruption, and this mortal must put on immortality. So when this corruptible shall have put on incorruption, and this mortal shall have put on immortality, then shall be brought to pass the saying that is written, Death is swallowed up in victory. O death, where is thy sting? O grave, where is thy victory? (1 Corinthians 15:51–55 KJV).

Lazarus

And whatsoever ye shall ask in my name, that will I do, that the Father may be glorified in the Son. If ye shall ask anything in my name, I will do (1John 14:13, 14 KJV).

As I picked up the call from the emergency department I heard muffled whispering on the other end of the line. "We have a potential problem down here," said one of the RNs working the 11-7 shift. When I asked her if I needed to come down, she said that things were under control at the moment, but she wasn't sure what was going to happen.

A 64-year-old man had arrived dead on arrival (DOA) after suffering a cardiac arrest at home. CPR and artificial ventilations had been performed for more than 30 minutes with no response. The man was pronounced dead in the ED about 10 minutes after his arrival there. The family arrived immediately after the patient, as did the patient's minister.

According to the RN who had paged me, the minister and family members had begun praying loudly, commanding the man to rise up from the dead. Because of the content and volume of the prayers, the expired patient, his family and the minister were moved to a private room. It was the hope of the nursing staff that the yelling and praying would not be a disturbance to the other ED patients.

"They are calling forth this man from the dead as if he were Lazarus. Some lady is praying and talking in another language. It's kind of freaky. I respect people's religious beliefs, but I'm afraid these people are going to get out of hand. I'll call you if they become a problem," said the ED nurse before hanging up the phone.

Respecting other people's religious beliefs is not usually hard for most nurses to do, unless those religious beliefs vary from the expected norm. Such was the case with the minister and group of family members who were yelling and calling this dead man to awaken and rise up. The "speaking in tongues" was also not something seen or heard before by the majority of people present in the ED that night.

The vigil with the expired patient went on for about four or five hours. "They just won't give up and accept the fact that the man is dead," said one of the nurses.

The staff and other patients in the ED that night didn't understand the yelling or the "speaking in tongues." They had a hard time believing that someone could be prayed back to life.

"Wouldn't it be a wonderful thing for this man to wake up and live again? Maybe people would believe in God and His ability to perform miracles through His chosen people." Those were my thoughts as I made my rounds. I had many questions that night. "Where was the faith of these praying Christians? Where was the power behind their prayers? Where was God? Why didn't He raise this man from the dead and prove that He is a God of miracles, that nothing is impossible with Him? Was it not His will that this man return to life? Why don't Christians have the power within them that was promised to those who have the indwelling of the Holy Spirit?

The disciples traveled with Christ and saw Him perform numerous healings and miracles. They saw Him cast out evil spirits and raise people from death. In one instance, the disciples were unable to cast out the evil spirits. They couldn't understand why Christ could do the miraculous and they couldn't. He had told them that they would be able to perform the same healings and miracles as he performed.

When Christ saw their inability to cast out the evil spirits, He said to them, "Howbeit this kind goeth not out but by prayer and fasting" (Matthew 17:21 KJV). Christ said that they would be able to perform the same miracles and healings that He performed, but that they had to be in a spiritual place with Him for this to happen.

John 14:12 (KJV) states, "Verily, verily, I say unto you, He that believeth on me, the works that I do shall he do also; and greater works than these shall he do; because I go unto my Father." In this scripture, Jesus is speaking. He tells His disciples that they and those who believe on Him will have the power and ability to heal, perform miracles, raise the dead and cast out evil spirits just like He did. In fact, they will perform greater miracles or works after Jesus leaves them.

The minister and family of the deceased man went home approximately five hours after the patient was pronounced dead. The patient went to the morgue. I wondered about the minister's feelings of failure when he was not able to pray the man back to life. Did he wonder why his prayers were not answered? Did he wonder where God was? Did he lose his faith? Did he wonder about the promise of God, "And whatsoever ye shall ask in my name, that will I do, that the Father may be glorified in the Son. If ye shall ask anything in my name, I will do it" (John 14:13, 14 KJV)?

To see miracles happen, we must ask ourselves, "Do I really believe? Do I have faith to believe it can or will happen? Is it God's will for it to occur?"

There is nothing that discourages or decreases faith more than for a fervent, faith-filled prayer to go unanswered. This minister and the family members went out on a limb by exercising their faith. They put themselves out there and set themselves up to be seen as crazy religious fanatics by the world around them. So why didn't Christ honor their prayers and raise the man from the dead?

God does answer our many prayers. The reason why He doesn't answer all prayers, especially ones where Christians fervently pray and believe for a miracle, is known only by Him. I do know that He is in control, and He answers prayers according to His will and His purpose. He commands us to fast and pray if we want to see the miraculous. I wonder what kind of "God" things we would see if we were obedient to his command to fast and pray?

Rhea

...then shall be brought to pass the saying that is written, Death is swallowed up in victory. O death, where is thy sting? O grave, where is thy victory? (1 Corinthians 15:54-55 KJV).

Rhea was sure that she would beat the disease that attacked suddenly and with a viciousness that startled not only her, but the medical team, as well. The brain tumor manifested itself one weekend in November. At first Rhea complained of a dull headache that would disappear for a few hours after taking a mild pain reliever. The headache would reoccur three to four hours later. As the headaches became more severe, they also increased in frequency.

The last night I worked with Rhea, she started crying and said, "There is something wrong with me. I can't remember little things. I'm really scared."

The nurses working that night did not take Rhea's fears seriously. We told her that it was probably stress and hormones related to her age. We didn't worry until Sunday evening. Rhea was scheduled to work the 7 p.m. to 7 a.m. shift and didn't show up for report. She was found driving around in the hospital parking lot. She was unable to remember why she was at the hospital. It was now evident that Rhea had reason for her fears.

Rhea was taken into the emergency unit. When a CT scan of the brain was done, it revealed an abnormal growth, or tumor, in her head. Rhea was sent to a metropolitan hospital about 60 miles away for brain surgery. The morbid diagnosis of gliobastoma, a frequently fatal type of brain tumor, was given. Rhea underwent brain surgery, followed by chemotherapy and radiation of the malignant tumor.

Nothing worked! Tomorrow my friend Rhea is being buried. She was 48-years-old when she found out that she had a malignant brain tumor. She was diagnosed a little over six months ago and now she is gone. Rhea left behind a beautiful 15-year-old daughter and a husband that she adored. Rhea loved her family and talked about them everyday at work.

After reading her obituary in the newspaper, I was reminded of the wedding vows that are said by the bride and the groom: "…for better, for worse, for richer, for poorer, in sickness and in health, to love and to cherish; till death do us part." There was little resemblance to the Rhea in the obituary and the Rhea I saw lying in the hospice unit on the day of her death. That is what terminal disease and its treatment will do to a person. It steals their life and there is little resemblance to the person that they used to be. That did not matter to Rhea's family. They stayed with her until she stopped living.

Rhea and I had talked about life here and life after death about four months ago. She looked at me from her hospital bed and said, "I'm not afraid to die. I'm ready to go, but what about my daughter and my husband? I'm afraid for them. What will they do without me? What will my daughter do without her mom?"

The questions were sobering and hard. I had no answer for Rhea. All that I could do was hold onto her hand and tell her that I'd be praying not only for her recovery, but for strength for her family. Rhea died without the ability to remember our conversation. She didn't know most of us during her last few months of life. Because of the location of the brain tumor, she was unable to remember even her own family.

During Rhea's illness, I wrote a letter to a minister friend. I told her that Rhea's terminal diagnosis and resulting death affected me more than any that I've had to experience. Her illness and subsequent death has caused me to stop and question my faith and my purpose. Why write stories about hope and healing when I see people dying all around? They suffer and then they die. I see people healed, but it seems that there are more people who die from the many diseases that plague society today. I have become morbid in my thinking and I wonder where hope has gone.

Then I was reminded of Christ's promise. Eugene H. Peterson's "The Message" (the Bible in contemporary language) describes death in 1 Thessalonians, Chapter 14: "And regarding the question, friends, that has come up about what happens to those already dead and buried, we don't want you in the dark any longer. First off, you must not carry on over them like people who have nothing to look forward to, as if the grave were the last word. Since Jesus died and broke loose from the grave, God will most certainly bring back to life those who died in Jesus."

> *Behold, I shew you a mystery: We shall not all sleep but we shall all be changed, In a moment, in the twinkling of an eye, at the last trump: for the trumpet shall sound, and the dead shall be raised incorruptible, and we shall be changed. ... then shall be brought to pass the saying that is written, Death is swallowed up in victory. O death, where is thy sting? O grave, where is thy victory?* (1 Corinthians 15:51-55 KJV).

After reading these promises of life after this short time on earth, how can I not have hope when I know that death and the grave are not final? Life will go on for those who believe in God and His Son. There will be new life for those who believe that Jesus died as the sacrifice for their sins. He died to give hope after life and death.

Divine Appointment

And let us not be weary in well doing: for in due season we shall reap, if we faint not. As we have therefore opportunity, let us do good unto all men, especially unto them who are of the household of faith (Galatians 6:9, 10 KJV).

While reading a book that talked about God's intervention in all aspects of life, the words *Divine appointment* caught my attention. Suddenly it all made sense. God has been scheduling these divine appointments nearly every day of my life.

"Why would I run into that one person who is having the same problem that I just went through? Why would I be assigned to care for this patient who has the exact diagnosis as the woman in the article I had just read . . . the same woman who had survived a terminal disease?" I asked these questions and ones like them many times over the years. Most of the time, I blamed the encounter on coincidence. But I've learned that coincidence is nothing more than God's divine appointment. Situations that were arranged by God to put me in a certain place at a certain time with a certain individual. This is how I would define the phrase *divine appointment.*

It is usually during these divine appointments that I feel God nudging me to do or say something to someone who is in need or someone who is in the middle of a life-changing situation. These life-changing situations may be times of illness or great loss. Sometimes, these situations are times of great celebration or mountain top experiences.

Whatever the backdrop for the divine appointment, I always know in my spirit that I am where I am for a reason. That reason is not happenstance or chance. It is a God-appointed meeting.

I would like to say that I have always been obedient and done exactly what God required of me during these divine appointments, but I haven't always done the right thing when these situations were presented to me.

About 15 years ago, I was working in the Intensive Care Unit (ICU) of a small community hospital in western Pennsylvania. My scheduled shift was 7 p.m. to 7 a.m. and I worked three days a week. I loved the job. The people in this small town were friendly, kind and hard-working. Most of the nursing staff came from the area. Therefore, they knew the patients who came into our unit. I had just moved from Houston, Texas and didn't know anybody.

Houston is a diverse and transient city. Despite its size and population, it was a friendly place. People were smiling and kind but more on a superficial level because of the fast pace and stressful daily grind. So it was refreshing to work in a small town hospital again where the nursing staff not only knew each other, but they knew the patients, and the patients' parents, grandparents, children and grandchildren.

One Saturday evening, I was assigned to care for Mrs. Jones. She was a 70-year-old woman who had severe heart disease. Her heart muscle had been damaged to the point that it was too weak to circulate the blood in her body without the use of several medications. This woman needed a heart transplant, but because of her age and debilitated condition, she was not a candidate for a new heart.

Mrs. Jones was a stuffy, arrogant, non-smiling woman who had little family or friends to support her. Her only visitor was one daughter that she still acknowledged as a family member. Her other children were estranged, as were most of her neighbors and friends. Mrs. Jones was demanding, nasty and downright mean most of the time. She didn't like chit-chat or small talk. She wanted what she wanted right now.

Mrs. Jones usually got what she wanted because her daughter was one of the administrators of the hospital. None of the nurses wanted to care for Mrs. Jones. She was a difficult and nasty lady, but because of her daughter's position in the hospital, the staff had to keep their mouths shut and take the abuse that she dished out.

Many times, I wanted to let Mrs. Jones know how I felt about her insults and her demands, but I just turned and walked out of the room instead of opening my mouth. My tongue was about bitten off by the end of the first evening.

When I went in the room to care for Mrs. Jones, I tried to be optimistic and encouraging. Entering the room that evening, I smiled and introduced myself. Mrs. Jones just stared at me like I had three heads. She demanded some small task of me, then turned her head toward the wall and closed her eyes. I decided that I was not going to react to Mrs. Jones' dismissal of my care and presence like I wanted to react.

Going through my mind repeatedly was the statement, "Unlovable people are the ones who really need love." Mrs. Jones definitely belonged in the unlovable category. She didn't even try to let people love her. She didn't care whether people liked her or not.

During the divine appointment with Mrs. Jones that Saturday night, God must have given me an overflow of empathy, mercy and grace. For a few brief moments, He let me see through His eyes the pain and fear of this lonely woman who was destined to die very soon.

So I put on my smile and patiently took her verbal abuse as I cared for her. At one point, I went into the room and just sat in the chair beside her bed. She had her eyes closed and her head turned toward the wall. I took her hand, and she quickly turned to me. With an icy stare that pierced to the heart, she looked from me to her hand. Telling her that I sensed that she was afraid, angry and in pain, I offered her my presence and my ear if she wanted to talk. She stared at me for a few long seconds. I just met her stare. For a few brief seconds, I saw her eyes soften and tear up before she turned her head back to the wall.

"I'm all right!" she said. Leaving her hand in mine, I wondered how long it had been since she felt someone touch her. She definitely was not the touchable type.

"Well, God, You put me here for some reason," I prayed. "Give me the words to say to help this miserable woman."

No words came, so I sat with Mrs. Jones for several minutes. I won't say that she and I became fast friends, but she did start acting a little nicer to me. She even started making sarcastic comments to my questions. I realized that under all that defensive outer shell of meanness was a bright and funny lady. The mean and nasty behavior kept people away. It kept people from seeing how afraid and how sad she really was on the inside.

Mrs. Jones spent about a week in our ICU. I cared for her on the days that I worked. She eventually opened up a little, and we talked about life, death and what came next. Mrs. Jones was agnostic and had no belief in a God of any kind. She had no belief in the afterlife. Her comment to me when I talked to her about the subject was, "When I'm gone, I'm gone. There is nothing else. That's it."

Mrs. Jones said these things with such finality and feeling that I cut short our divine appointment. I knew that God had placed me with this bitter, mean woman so I could encourage her and tell her about the hope of something better after her short life here on earth. When I said the word heaven, she gave me that daggers-type stare. So I stopped talking.

Leaving that night, I knew that I should have told Mrs. Jones about a God who loved her just the way she was. I should have told her about God's forgiveness of sin and about a relationship with Him here on earth. I should have told her how much she was loved and that she was never really alone. I should have told her about the hope for something better after this life. But I didn't. She didn't want to hear it; and because of her daughter's position as administrator, I knew that I could lose my job. As a staff nurse, I was not permitted to pray with my patients, nor was I permitted to talk to them about God's love and hope for their future.

Isn't that the most ironically stupid thing? People who are dying, those who are in constant pain and those who are fearful are the very people who need to hear about hope, not just in this world but about hope in life after death.

After leaving work that morning, I berated myself the whole way home because I didn't do what I knew God had appointed me to do. I didn't sleep much that day. Mrs. Jones' face would appear, and I would see her anger and her pain. Then I would hear her words, "When I'm gone, I'm gone."

Having asked for forgiveness for not being obedient during this divine appointment, I made the promise to God that when I went into work that evening, I would talk to Mrs. Jones about His love, forgiveness, heaven and hope after this life. I decided that if I lost my job, then so be it. I would keep my divine appointment; it would just be a little late.

That night, I walked into the unit and went to Mrs. Jones' room. The room was dark, the bed made up. There was nobody in the room. When I went to the desk to ask if she had been transferred out of the ICU, I knew without waiting for the answer that I had missed my divine appointment with Mrs. Jones. She had died during the day. At around the same time that I was promising God that I would make another "appointment" with Mrs. Jones and say what should have been said the previous evening, she died in the ICU.

Cold fear gripped me. Was I responsible for her dying and not ever hearing the salvation message? Did she die with no hope? Did she think about the few things that I had told her about God and His love? I had been given a divine appointment and had not kept it as I should have.

I learned a valuable and sobering lesson that night. Those who I meet with or talk with may have no other opportunity to hear the message of hope and healing on earth, of heaven and eternal life. I've learned since that day to take divine appointments seriously. They are not just coincidental encounters. It may be the last chance somebody has to hear about and find Christ.

My Healing

Insomuch that the multitude wondered, when they saw the dumb to speak, the maimed to be whole, the lame to walk, and the blind to see: and they glorified the God of Israel (Matthew 15:31 KJV).

My Healing From Multiple Sclerosis
Written by Doug Leighty

On June 20, 2005, I was diagnosed as having Multiple Sclerosis (MS). My health had gradually deteriorated over the years. Looking back on it now, I can see that the effects of the disease started as early as 1997. In June of 2005, my wife insisted that I go to our family doctor and find out what was wrong with me. The doctor ordered an MRI of my brain, which eventually confirmed his suspicions. At his suggestion, I went to Johns Hopkins in Baltimore for a second opinion in August of 2005. My neurologist there is Justin McArthur. He is a Professor of Neurology at The Johns Hopkins University School of Medicine, as well as being an author and researcher. At my visit there, he immediately agreed with the diagnosis and stated, "You definitely have MS. No doubt about it." He put my MRI up to the light. "See those spots there and there and there? That's classic MS. This is what I would show to my students."

So now we had the reason behind the symptoms. The symptoms were getting worse as time went on. I had to walk with my feet wide apart to compensate for my balance problems. My right calf muscle was barely working. I could no longer point my right foot up toward my knee. I couldn't walk in a normal heel-to-toe fashion with my right leg. So walking consisted of limping as I stepped with my left leg and swinging my right leg in front of me. Limp, swing, limp, swing, step after step, day after day.

I had chronic fatigue. When I woke up in the morning, it was like I never went to bed. It became difficult to shower because the ten minutes or so that it took to shower was my limit for standing up. If I tried to go outside and play in the front yard with my son, I couldn't do much; and after five or ten minutes, I would have to go in and collapse on the couch. I fell asleep pretty much anywhere because I was so tired all the time, but I never felt rested. At a Johns Hopkins follow-up visit in September of 2006, I was evaluated at "4" on the Expanded Disability Status Scale (EDSS). This is a standard

MS disability scale of 1 to 10, with 10 being the worst.

I had an action tremor in my right hand. When I tried to use my hand, it would shake uncontrollably. I had to eat and drink with my left hand. Writing a complete sentence with a pen or pencil was absolutely exhausting. For the most part, I stopped playing the piano, which I had done previously for about the last 30 years. The tremor took away my finger precision, so I couldn't hit the keys that I needed to when I needed to.

I had a constant headache. When I took Excedrin, it dulled the pain for four hours, but the pain never went away. Dr. McArthur put me on Topamax to try to control the tremor, and this doubled as a headache medicine. It did make the pain more bearable, but, again, the headache never went away.

I had no appetite. One Johns Hopkins report said that I was about 20 pounds underweight. My height is a little over 5'10", but my weight had gotten as low as 132 pounds. My wife described me as "gaunt." And she was right.

I fell down on a regular basis. If I would start to fall, my legs didn't work well enough for me to catch myself. I had problems with balance because of the MS, so falling down was pretty easy for me to do. There was no falling with style. I would either hit the floor with a thud or crash into and through whatever was nearby.

I was grumpy, miserable, and depressed. Life had become overwhelming. I cried a lot, even about little things that didn't really matter at all.

In February of 2006, I began taking an interferon called Rebif. This medicine is a shot delivered by self-injection. I was taking this three times a week. This was not really something that I wanted to do, but I did it out of a sense of responsibility to my family. Rebif is not a cure for MS. It is designed to reduce the number and frequency of the brain lesions that are a part of MS. The medicine doesn't prevent MS disabilities. It just slows down getting there.

From the day of the diagnosis, I believed God would heal me. I described myself as having a "temporarily incurable" disease. There were struggles and discouragement along the way as I waited for the healing to come. Still, I dreamed of what it would be like to be well again. On October 26, 2006, God gave me my miracle.

Our home church, Christ Community Church in Camp Hill, Pennsylvania, was hosting a three-night conference called "Naturally Supernatural." The speaker was Pastor Che Ahn from Harvest Rock Church in Los Angeles. One of his associate pastors, Steven Hagashi, was also there for the conference. On the second night, Pastor Hagashi prayed for me at the end of the service. It was a good prayer, but there weren't any lightning bolts or anything. I went home, took my Rebif shot and went to bed.

The next day, October 27, I went to work. As I walked from the car to my building, I noticed something strange. I was feeling the muscles on the insides of my thighs as I walked. Then I noticed why. I was walking with my feet at normal width, not the wide gait to which I had become accustomed. As the day went on, my walking got stronger. I would get up from my desk and walk to the restroom, just because I was amazed that I was walking heel-to-toe on my right leg. It was a wonderful feeling. I was still trying to come to grips with what was happening to me. I stood up in my office cubicle and looked to make sure nobody was around. Then I tried jumping. I actually got off the ground (not very high) and landed without falling or even losing my balance. At this point, my hope was soaring. I didn't want to jump to conclusions, but I knew things were incredibly different.

I held my right hand out in front of me. I moved it around and waited for the tremor to begin. It didn't. My heart was beating faster as I sat and stared at my hand. By the end of the day, I absolutely knew that God had healed me.

When I got home, I had a great time telling everyone what happened. There was much rejoicing at what God had done for me.

It wasn't until the next day, October 28, that I noticed that my headache was gone. It was a completely new and wonderful sensation. My head had hurt for so long, it became what was normal.

Now, there was no pain. None! Living without a headache was virtually unimaginable to me, but now it was a reality.

My wife and I went shopping that Saturday. I walked as we shopped for about an hour. Before my healing, I had to have a motorized cart anytime I went shopping. Without it, I would have to just sit somewhere most of the time. Now, I was walking and standing. The fatigue that had prevented me from doing so many things was gone.

I've started exercising again, which had become almost impossible to do. At this writing, it has been about ten weeks since I was healed. I'm still doing fine and getting stronger. I can run some now, but I'm still working at getting stronger in my ankles. A few weeks ago, my son and I played catch with the softball for approximately 20 minutes. He wore out before I did.

I can play the piano again. This has been a large part of my life. To have it taken away was devastating. To have it back is a magnificent gift.

Since my healing, I've gained about 12 pounds. My appetite has returned, and eating is a pleasure again instead of a chore. I'm well on my way to a healthy, normal weight.

I had a follow-up at Johns Hopkins this week. Dr. McArthur's reaction to all of this was, "Well, I wish we could take credit for this, but we really can't." He also said that he wouldn't normally recommend stopping Rebif for someone with brain lesions, but he understands that I'm coming at this thing from a different direction. I haven't taken any Rebif or Topamax since October 27, 2006.

Some of this story is still being written. I haven't had a new MRI yet, but that will happen this summer. I'm confident that this will show more of what God did in me.

God has changed my life in so many ways, large and small, with this healing. I give Him all thanks and praise. My gratitude goes beyond what I can express in words.

I do not have MS anymore!

Verily, verily, I say unto you, He that believeth on me, the works that I do shall he do also; and greater works than these shall he do; because I go unto my Father. And whatsoever ye shall ask in my name, that will I do, that the Father may be glorified In the Son (John 14:12, 13 KJV).

Defying Death

That your faith should not stand in the wisdom of men, but in the power of God (1 Corinthians 2:5 KJV).

The following story is from an ICU experience approximately five years ago. I was working a 16-hour shift one Saturday. It was my turn to take the next admission. When I got the assignment and report, I knew that it was going to be an emotional evening. My assigned patient was Mr. Smith, a 76-year-old gentleman who had suffered a massive stroke confirmed by a head CT. He arrived on the unit around 3 p.m.

Mr. Smith was an active man who had a wife, four adult children and several grandchildren. He was very close to his family even though three of his children lived in different states. Mr. Smith was an avid gardener and kept busy all hours of the day. His wife said that he could not relax and just sit around; he had to be doing something.

When Mr. Smith suffered his stroke, he had a large amount of bleeding into the brain, and this resulted in a respiratory arrest. Because of the neurological symptoms and the CT results, the family was given the news that the condition was grave. Mr. Smith was having seizures almost continuously. His heart rate and blood pressure were unstable, and the family was told that he would not live through the night.

Mrs. Smith asked me to please keep her husband alive until her other three children could come to say goodbye. One daughter lived close by, and she remained at her father's side. Mrs. Smith called a son in Delaware, a daughter in New Jersey, and another son in Virginia. She asked us to do whatever we needed to do to keep him alive until his children arrived.

Around 5 p.m., two hours after admission, I was hanging the fifth intravenous medications to stabilize Mr. Smith's rhythm and blood pressure. Mr. Smith continued to have frequent seizures and was breathing with the assistance of a ventilator. Mrs. Smith and her daughter stayed in the room and kept in constant contact with the other children.

At one point in the evening, Mrs. Smith asked me to pray with her. She asked me to pray that Mr. Smith would awake and be well; but if he had to die, that he would live long enough for his children to arrive to say goodbye. When I asked her how long before everyone would arrive, she said it would take approximately seven hours. I prayed with Mrs. Smith, asking God to stabilize Mr. Smith's blood pressure and heart rhythm so he would live through the night.

About ten minutes after our prayer, Mr. Smith's heart rate dropped to 40, then 30, and then asystole or no cardiac activity at all. Mr. Smith arrested, and the Cardiac Arrest Team (CAT) was called. The arrest team arrived and worked on Mr. Smith for about 20 minutes. Because of the bleeding into his brain, it was determined that Mr. Smith would never awaken from a coma even if we would get his heart rhythm back to normal. After talking with Mrs. Smith, the emergency doctor called the code (stopped all resuscitation measures) and pronounced Mr. Smith dead.

Because Mr. Smith was my patient, it was my responsibility to clean his body and remove all the lines and tubes. Everyone had left the room, and as I started removing things, I prayed for Mr. Smith to get a rhythm back and live long enough for his children to arrive to say their goodbyes. Normally after a patient dies, the nurse removes the EKG leads and turns the monitor off. I had not removed the EKG leads yet, but I had turned off the monitor in the room. As I was beginning to remove the endotracheal (breathing) tube, the other nurses came running into the room.

"What are you doing in here?" asked one of the nurses. Turning around, I told her I was taking out the lines and cleaning Mr. Smith. One of the nurses turned on the monitor, and when I looked up at it, I got chills. Mr. Smith had a heart rhythm. As I watched, the rate increased from 30 to about 50. "It's just the epinephrine effect," said one of the nurses. But when I checked for a pulse I felt one in his carotid artery. The ventilator was turned back on to give oxygen to Mr. Smith. As we stood in the room watching the monitor, we all realized that Mr. Smith did not have a heart rhythm because of epinephrine. Mr. Smith had a heart rhythm and a pulse because he was alive. Mr. Smith, who had been pronounced dead a few minutes before, had a pulse and a normal heart rhythm!

At 10:30 p.m., all four of Mr. Smith's children walked into the room. Mrs. Smith smiled at me as we acknowledged the fact that God had answered her prayer. Mr. Smith had been pronounced dead and had a return of his heart rhythm. He lived until his entire family arrived to tell him goodbye.

Mr. Smith died around 2 a.m. His family was at his side and said their goodbyes. He didn't get well and make it out of the hospital, but God performed a miracle in allowing him to live long enough for his family to say goodbye. In fact, Mr. Smith lived for eight hours after being pronounced dead.

Dysfunctional

Peace I leave with you, my peace I give unto you: not as the world giveth, give I unto you. Let not your heart be troubled neither let it be afraid (John 14:27 KJV).

The young woman's name was Erin. She was a 35-year-old wife and mother of two children. Her son was eleven and her daughter eight years old. Erin came into the ICU one evening after having undergone radical abdominal surgery. The surgery was performed as an emergent effort to save Erin's life. She had a self-inflicted gun shot wound to the abdomen. Whatever her intent, Erin did not succeed in dying as a consequence of her actions. The bullet missed her aorta, which would have caused death by blood loss within seconds of firing the gun. The bullet missed her spine, the result which could have been paralysis. It missed her lungs, heart, pancreas, kidneys, and stomach. If the bullet had hit any of these major organs, her chance of survival would have been greatly diminished. Erin shot herself at such an angle that her small intestine was hit as was her liver. After major surgery, a portion of the bowel and damaged liver were removed. Erin ended up with a bowel resection and colostomy, but her life was saved—much to her dismay.

Erin had been an alcoholic for more than ten years. She was unable to keep a job. She had very few friends, and her extended family had all but deserted her because of her alcohol-related problems.

Erin arrived on the unit that night around 8 p.m. I helped get her settled into the bed after her surgery. She was hooked to a ventilator, which assisted her to breathe. She had tubes and lines everywhere. Drains, EKG cables, intravenous lines and ventilator tubing covered her small, 90-pound frame. For two days, Erin did well until she began to have symptoms of alcohol withdrawal, Delirium Tremors (D.T.s). Erin's D.T.s began on her second post-operative night.

She spent almost three weeks in ICU as a result of the alcohol withdrawal. She required an extra week of ventilator support with heavy sedation to stabilize her condition. She hallucinated, seeing bugs and snakes on the walls and floors. She was angry, confused and delirious for most of the three weeks. She ripped off her dressings and tore out drains and IV lines. She even attempted to remove her own breathing tube. For more than a week, Erin required a continuous sitter to keep her from harming herself.

Once she was off the ventilator, Erin refused to talk about the fact that she tried to end her life. She was an angry and addicted woman who gave little thought to her husband and children who stayed by her side. Erin's son and daughter tried to get her attention when they entered the room after the breathing tube had been removed. Even after no contact with her children for nearly three weeks, Erin seemed annoyed by their efforts to reach out to her. She wouldn't hug or kiss her children when they attempted to come to her. Instead, she yelled at them and pushed them away. I wondered about the dysfunctional home life of those two little children. They lived with a father who worked every day trying to make a normal life for his family, all the while dealing with an alcohol addicted wife who put no effort into mothering her own two children.

Erin lived a life of torment. She was the prisoner of addiction, like so many others in society today. She couldn't deal with her life anymore and by killing herself, she thought that she could escape the pain and addiction to alcohol. It seemed to be the only answer to obtain peace. The alcohol worked for the first few years but heavier doses of the drug were needed to give her that peaceful feeling. Erin was addicted and she was not at peace. She made the decision that she wouldn't live as an addict any longer. She was destroying her heath, her marriage and her family. She just wanted it all to end.

Erin's attempts to end it all failed. She now must face life again with or without the assistance of alcohol. She has made it through the physical addiction but now must deal with the emotional aspects of alcohol withdrawal. She left the ICU having gone three weeks without it, but her frame of mind remained that of a surly, angry and anxious woman.

Delirium Tremors is a serious and sometimes fatal condition that is the result of alcohol withdrawal. The patients are younger and have crossed the predominant male gender line over the past several years. It used to be that the average age and sex of the patient experiencing D.T.s was a 65-year-old male.

The age and the gender of the patient with D.T.s has changed. More and more hospital personnel see young men and women with alcohol addictions. Many of these alcohol dependent people can go on for years with no symptoms of alcoholism. There may be no indication that the person has an alcohol problem until the alcohol is suddenly removed from the system for a couple of days.

Last night, I was called to start two IVs. The calls came, requesting a "stat" response. Both IVs needed to be inserted as soon as possible because both patients were experiencing symptoms of D.T.s. Both women had become agitated and ripped out their previous IV lines. In both cases, the doctor had ordered IV medication to help calm the patient and prevent full-blown D.T.s, which can result in seizures and death. One of the female patients was a 33-year-old. The other woman was 41 years old.

At least once a week, I am called to start an IV on a patient who has D.T.s. These patients have gone around 48 hours without alcohol. Every patient who is admitted to the hospital is asked, "Do you drink alcohol, and if so, how much?" It has been determined that if the patient says one or two drinks a day, then that usually means two to four drinks a day. Some patients will admit to a six pack or two per day or a fifth every couple of days. Even though the patient may say one or two beers a day, the nursing staff has learned to assess for signs and symptoms of D.T.s. This is done on all patients, but especially on patients who will be in the hospital for more than 48 hours.

A few months ago, as I made rounds in the ICU, eight out of nine patients were exhibiting signs and symptoms of D.T.s. During the post-operative course, D.T.s is significant enough to cause the patient to be intubated and placed on a ventilator with heavy sedation. Most patients with D.T.s will hallucinate and become increasingly confused and delusional. They are anxious and attempt to climb out of bed. The typical patient with D.T.s is often mean and belligerent, and will strike out at those around him or her.

It is not an easy job caring for the alcohol-addicted patient in D.T.s. The patient's heart rate is elevated as is the blood pressure. Sometimes, this elevation is at a dangerous level. The patient's temperature rises. Tremors of the hands, arms and the entire body occur. If not controlled, the patient can develop seizures that are life-threatening. Confusion, paranoia, anxiety and hallucinations come next. The patient acts out and endangers not only him or her self, but the staff providing care can also be at risk.

There are so many people living with anxiety and stress. They are looking for a way to deal with life. They need a way to relieve the worry and pain of living. It makes me wonder about what my own addictions might be except for the peace that I have found in knowing God personally. He promises a peace that passes all understanding. That is true peace! Many times, when I am anxious, in emotional pain or worried to the point of irrational thought, I have only to call out to God and ask for peace. He has never failed me. A calm feeling comes over me like a warm blanket, and I know in my soul that things will be okay regardless of what goes on around me. This peace that passes all understanding takes the place of the peace that is often found with alcohol or drugs. The difference is that the peace of God lasts where the peace found in a substance is short lived.

> *These things I have spoken unto you, that in me ye might have peace. In the world ye shall have tribulation: but be of good cheer; I have overcome the world* (John 16:33 KJV).

Special Needs

Blessed are the poor in spirit: for theirs is the kingdom of heaven (Matthew 5:3 KJV).

Johney was first introduced to me on a cool, spring morning in May. I had been working at the facility for about a week when one of the nurses decided it was time to take me around to meet the residents, most of whom were elderly. Many were confused and didn't remember anything about our conversation two minutes after I walked away. Nearly all of the residents were hard of hearing, and there wasn't a person in the place who didn't wear glasses and dentures.

Johney was the exception. He was blind and didn't need the glasses. He was deaf and mute. Johney was 14 years old when I first met him. He had spent the past eight years of his life in the facility. Johney had been born with cerebral palsy. He had the mental capacity and bodily function of an infant and he was unable to walk or talk. Because of severe curvature of his spine, Johney had a hunched-back appearance. He had deformities of both legs, which were spindly and short. His arms were contracted, and he was unable to open his hands unless the staff pried his fingers out of their curled fist-like position. Johney was fed from a tube four times a day and had been since birth. Because of a congenital heart defect, Johney frequently had bouts of congestive heart failure. Because of his weakened heart muscle, his body fluid would back up into his lungs and he would cough until he turned purple.

Johney weighed in excess of 180 pounds. He was unable to move on his own. Because of an abnormal growth spurt, Johney became too large for his parents to care for. When he was six years old, his family was forced to place him in the nursing facility. Because of his immobility and his size, two people were needed to move Johney from chair to bed and to properly position him.

There were many days when I would hear Johney coughing from my office two halls away. His cough was high-pitched, shrill and constant. We all knew that because of the intensity of the cough, Johney was getting no air during the coughing jags. Activity would stop in the halls, and no noise was heard. Everyone waited for Johney to stop coughing and take in a gulp of air. When the coughing stopped, whether on its own or with the help of positioning and suctioning by staff members, we all breathed a sigh of relief.

Johney became everyone's little boy even though he was 14 years old. Caring for Johney was like caring for a large infant. Sometimes, the staff would let him taste certain liquids or foods that would not require chewing. Johney would scrunch up his face and make sucking noises. He would then open his mouth and eyes wide wanting more. Johney was very ticklish, and one of the nurses, Carla, would make him giggle by poking him in the belly or by tickling his chin. Johney would break out in a big smile, and his whole body would shake in giggles. Hearing Johney laugh was one of the sounds that made my day.

There is not a lot of happiness or laughter in a nursing home. Many of the residents are too confused to know where they are living. The ones that know where they are realize that this is their last home. Most have been sent to this place to die. So the atmosphere is heavy with depression, and many times, shame. There is embarrassment over not being able to remember people or recognize names. There is the shame caused by incontinence. There is also anger, bitterness and disappointment in the resident's family members who have "placed" their loved one in the facility only to return for sporadic visits.

So despite Johney's multiple problems and inability to communicate normally, he became the bright spot in many of the staff members' days. Johney was lifted in and out of bed each shift for a couple of hours. The staff would prop him up on numerous pillows and apply a seatbelt to keep him from toppling forward. Sitting Johney up in a chair was like trying to position a three month old infant. He couldn't even hold his head up, so the chair had to be reclined to keep him from toppling forward.

I used to spend my lunch hour walking the surrounding roads and facility grounds. There was a large lake on the front lawn. Many wild geese, ducks and swans walked the banks of the lake and surrounding lawn. That spring, I started taking Johney on my daily walk. After ensuring that Johney was secure in his wheelchair, we would go outside for a walk around the lake. The extended facility was quite large with the nursing home, a personal care facility and several small homes that encompassed a small village dedicated to the comfort and care of the elderly. There were many paved roads and paths meandering through the village. Johney and I would pass various staff members either taking a walk or running errands.

Pushing Johney in his wheelchair was quite a chore due to his excess weight. But when he and I would begin our walk, I quickly forgot about what a job it was to push him around. As soon as the breeze hit his face, Johney's features began to relax. He seemed to take a deep breath and sink into the chair, his face turned to the sun or breeze. He even loved to walk with the rain on his face on days when we didn't make it back inside to avoid the showers.

Johney and I always walked to the same spot on the lake. A gazebo had been built onto a deck that overlooked the lake. There were benches, a grill, picnic tables and a large tin container filled with food. It was beside the tin container that Johney and I would stop. I would take handfuls of the pellet-sized food and, after prying open his hand, would place the food in his fist. Together, we would throw the food into the lake. Immediately, the ducks and geese would fly, waddle or swim over for their lunch. Most of the birds were silent, but nearly every day there would be one selfish loudmouth goose that honked his way to the pellets. When the goose would make his annoying noise, Johney would stop moving and breathing. He would turn his ear to the sound of the goose fighting his way to the food. Then Johney would get a smile on his face. Did he hear the noisy goose? His medical records would say no. Johney was diagnosed as deaf. But sitting there with him while we fed the birds, I had no doubt that Johney heard the noise.

Johney and I would then turn around and walk back inside. Our return was always much slower because Johney loved the time spent outside of his four walls. When we returned to the room, the staff would pick him up and tuck him into his bed. He was asleep within minutes, a slight smile on his relaxed face. I like to imagine that he is dreaming of the lake and the birds, the feeling of the sun and breeze on his face. I also imagine that in the dream he gets up out of his chair and runs around the lake, chasing the swans and geese.

This story is dedicated to the administrators and staff of nursing homes and personal care homes everywhere. Your work is very seldom seen and appreciated by the general public, but your dedication and kindness will someday be rewarded. You are God's angels on earth.

Never Give Up

I call heaven and earth to record this day against you, that I have set before you life and death, blessing and cursing: therefore choose life, that both thou and thy seed may live (Deuteronomy 30:19 KJV).

As I write this story about Phil, I ask God to let the end be different from the other stories written about patients with stage-four cancers. In the other stories, the patients lived for only a short period of time and then died. These stories did not end with a miraculous recovery. Does this mean that the person had weak faith? Did those of us who prayed for the person have wavering faith? If so, then I ask God to increase my faith. I want to be able to pray for and believe in the miraculous healing of Phil's lung tumor and metastatic bone cancer.

"Wouldn't it be terrible to be a young man with two teenage children at home and be told that you are full of cancer?" This was the question asked by one of my coworkers after discussing Phil's diagnosis and treatment one evening almost three years ago. All of us who worked that evening had small children or teenagers at home. We all tried to imagine what it would be like to be given a death sentence like Phil had just been given. As I stared across the table at the other RNs working the evening shift, I silently prayed for wise words. I prayed for words that would let my coworkers know that there is still hope for Phil. I wanted to be able to express a hope that goes beyond what surgery, chemotherapy and radiation has to offer.

"Phil may experience a miracle. He believes that he will be healed." As I spoke these words, the nurses stared at me without a response. Phil believed in miracles. He was positive that he would beat this cancer. That doesn't mean that he is crazy. It means that he has faith.

As Phil spoke to me about his disease, he never moaned or complained even though the cancer in his spine made lying or sitting a painful experience. Phil talked about getting well, staying away from toxins that would deplete his immune system and about maintaining a positive attitude.

Phil had been diagnosed one-and-a-half years earlier with bone metastasis from his undiagnosed lung cancer. His chronic back pain suddenly became unbearable. Tumors were found in his lumbar spine. Because bone cancer is rarely the primary site, various scans were done and tissue tested to find the primary site of the cancer. By the time it was found in Phil's lung, the cancer had reached a stage four. Phil said that the cancer doctors just shook their heads and stated, "We can do palliative or comfort care only. Your cancer is too far advanced."

Phil's cancer had reached the final stages, and death was imminent. No cure exists for stage four lung cancer with metastatic disease. Phil had already tried various trials of chemotherapy and several weeks of radiation on the tumors in his lung and spine. He said that these treatments, combined with good food, rest, vitamins and a good attitude, would help him destroy the cancerous cells. He held on to his positive attitude and his faith that he would live.

I see people every day who have incurable and devastating diseases or addictions. Most have resigned themselves to the fact that there is no cure and no hope. They think they must live with the disease or addiction until death. Phil didn't see his disease that way. He said, "I have to keep a positive outlook about this. If I don't remain positive, then I have given up and the cancer will win."

Phil and I talked at length about the power of prayer and about God, who is able to deliver him from the cancer that is trying to destroy his body. Phil believes that God will heal him and that he will win this battle with cancer.

One-and-a-half years after first meeting Phil and three years after his initial diagnosis of stage four lung cancer, I saw him again in the cancer unit of the hospital. He wore a stocking cap because his hair was gone. When I walked in to talk with Phil, he was smiling and positive even though he was very weak after another bout of chemotherapy. He was still able to stand and walk, despite the nearly three years of metastatic spinal cancer. Phil has never given up hope and is still fighting a very courageous battle despite constant pain and weakness. As I talked to him, Phil still had a ready smile and a determination to beat the cancer.

That your faith should not stand in the wisdom of men, but in the power of God (1 Corinthians 2:5 KJV).

Dad

Is any among you afflicted? let him pray. Is any merry? Let him sing psalms. Is any sick among you? Let him call for the elders of the church; and let them pray over him, anointing him with oil in the name of the Lord: And the prayer of faith shall save the sick, and the Lord shall raise him up: and if he hath committed sins, they shall be forgiven him. (James 5:13-15 KJV).

Bonnie, my youngest sister, called me on a Saturday evening in April. She said, "Come over to Dad's house. Something is wrong. He's not talking right."

Slamming down the phone, I jumped up, grabbed my keys and ran out the door. As I made my way to the car, I yelled at everyone that I was going to Dad's house. "Something is wrong with him," I said. "It sounds like a stroke. Just pray for him!"

My Dad has always been my hero. Being one of three girls, I had the privilege of being the oldest and the favorite (or so he always made me feel like I was). I felt favored even though he was always fair and loving to us all. I'm sure my other two sisters thought that they were the favored ones, also. That's how he made us each feel. He taught us to hunt and fish, and change flat tires and the oil in the car. I remember lying under the car as he worked on the motor, transmission or muffler. He would patiently wait while I would hand him the various tools that he would ask for. Dad would always let my sisters and me help. He showed us the "how to" of everything he did. He even showed us how to shut down and start up a pumping machine for an oil well. Most people said he did all these things because he didn't have any boys to pass on this manly information to. But I know that he was trying to teach us everything that he could so we would grow to be autonomous women who didn't need to be dependent on anyone for survival.

Dad encouraged me and my sisters to go for whatever we wanted out of life. He told us that we could be whatever we wanted to be. If we worked hard and learned every aspect of the profession or job, then we would be able to rise to the top and manage the company we worked for. Better still, he taught us by experience that we could start our own company or business. His feeling was that if we were fair and honest, we would be successful at any job. His secret was to learn how to do every aspect of every job, be kind to people, be a team player rather than a dictator and don't let your life and business be motivated by the almighty dollar.

Dad was an entrepreneur. He had many businesses throughout his life. He never failed at any of them. He'd start the business, run it for awhile and then sell it for a profit. I watched him do this many times as I was growing up.

One thing that Dad always told us was, "Don't ever owe anyone anything. If someone needs your help, give it but don't take anything for it. Someday, you'll need their help, and there will always be people ready to give you a hand."

Mom and my two sisters, Tracey and Bonnie, would watch him help someone or fix something for people (he could fix anything). He'd sometimes be gone for hours. He'd never tell people no or that he was too busy. He always made time for anyone who asked. He would work for hours helping someone and he'd never take a cent. He'd say, "Someday, they'll pay me. I'll need their help someday."

My sisters and I used to get upset with him, saying things like, "You spent your entire Saturday doing something that would have cost that man a lot of money. You should charge something." Dad would just shrug and smile, saying, "Someday I'll collect."

Now that I'm older, I see his wisdom. He has 100 times more friends than most people his age. People just show up and do things for him and my mom. Or they just drop things off at his house. He knew what he was talking about all those years ago.

On this one particular Saturday, as I drove the three miles to his house, I thought of all the things that my Dad taught me over the years. Things like the way I should treat people and my work ethic. My parents never fought with people. If someone did something wrong to them, they would just walk away.

When I arrived at the house, my brother-in-law, Bob, a paramedic, had already done a head-to-toe neurological assessment. Bonnie, his wife, is an EMT and they both concurred with me that Dad's symptoms sounded like those of a stroke. The closest ambulance was 20 minutes away, so we made the decision to drive to the hospital ourselves. We loaded Dad into the van and pulled out of the driveway about ten minutes after his symptoms started.

Dad had receptive and expressive aphasia. He could not completely understand what was said to him and he couldn't say what he wanted to say.

After about 15 minutes, the receptive aphasia resolved, and he seemed to understand our questions. But when he would try to form a sentence, only one or two words made sense. The rest of the words were either garbled or inappropriate. Dad kept rubbing his right temple, saying he was having sharp pains from his ear to his head. He also said that he wasn't able to see things well. He would look at me and say, "The picture's wrong."

As a nurse in the ICU (Intensive Care Unit) caring for stroke patients, I realized that things could quickly get worse, especially if Dad had a bleeding vessel in his brain. We knew that we needed to get him to the ED quickly to get testing and treatment started. If the stroke was caused by a ruptured and bleeding blood vessel, the only treatment would be neurosurgery. This meant a helicopter trip to the nearest neurosurgeon, approximately 90 miles away. If the stroke was caused by a blood clot or a piece of plaque, medicine to dissolve the blockage would need to be given quickly. This would open up the blocked blood vessel and allow blood and oxygen to the tissue, thus preventing permanent damage to that area of the brain.

As we drove off to the hospital, I asked Bob to stop at our minister's house so he could pray for Dad. Bob wanted to get to the hospital as quickly as possible, but he also knows the power of effectual fervent prayer. God has the ultimate say as to the prognosis of a sick patient. So we made the stop at our pastor's home. As Dad sat in the van, Pastor Jack prayed for him and for his complete recovery from the problem.

My dad retired when he was 65 years old. He started playing the guitar at the same age. Being musically inclined, he learned quickly. Now eight years later, he travels three to four nights a week with a group of men and women who love to get together and play music. His band is asked to play for all types of social events. Sometimes, they just gather at each other's house and play for hours. The band frequently travels to retired communities and entertains the residents. Dad and his friends, most of whom are over 60 years of age, have their own private concert and party every Monday evening at Dad's house.

A stroke would have been devastating to my father, and his whole life would have been altered. That is the fact that made me fearful as I prayed for Dad's recovery. He is one of the happiest and busiest retired people I've ever seen. Working in the health care field, I've seen a lot of retired people who don't care about living any more.

When we arrived at the hospital, we rushed Dad into the ED and put him on a stretcher in the hall because the rooms were filled. Within ten minutes of lying down, Dad's verbal symptoms and mental confusion left. He has had no more stroke symptoms since that night.

Every test on the stroke protocol was done over the next two days. At age 73, it was declared that Dad was in excellent health. No cause for stroke or mini-stroke could be found. He was sent home on Plavix and Aspirin, two blood thinners. This was to prevent small blood clots from forming and going to the brain. This was one of the possible causes for the symptoms, although nothing was found.

Was it a real stroke or mini-stroke? None of the tests detected a problem. Even his normally elevated cholesterol was only slightly elevated. As health care workers, we sometimes have to shrug our shoulders and say, "I don't know why it happened. No cause could be found."

Dad definitely had symptoms of some type of neurological deficit that night. Was it the prayers of those around him who had faith to know that God will hear and answer all of our requests according to His divine purpose? I believe it to be so.

God hears and answers the prayers of His own. He has promised in His Word that He is the God. "Who forgiveth all thine iniquities; who healeth all thy diseases" (Psalms 103:3 KJV).

It is my sincere belief that Dad was healed that Saturday evening in April. God showed His favor and gave him a complete and irrevocable healing.

Obedience

For as by one man's disobedience many were made sinners, so by the obedience of one shall many be made righteous (Romans 5:19 KJV).

It was a beautiful Tuesday in September. Taylor, my youngest daughter, and I decided to go to Pittsburgh to meet her older sister and brother for lunch. Lexie and Blake were attending the University of Pittsburgh. They had not been home for a couple of weeks. Since Taylor and I were off for the day, we decided to go down and see them. We met at one of our favorite restaurants in Oakland, which sits right in the middle of the medical center.

As we sat talking, I kept glancing out the windows at the towering hospitals and medical buildings. Helicopters flew in and out of the University of Pittsburgh Medical Center (UPMC) in a constant stream. One of the hospitals was the trauma center, one was a children's specialty hospital and one was the Psychiatric Hospital of Western Pennsylvania. There was a hospital that specialized in cardiac disease, one that was geared to cancer patients and another was a woman's specialty center. There were a couple of general hospitals and several specialty clinics. Downtown Oakland, a suburb of Pittsburgh, has more hospitals and medical offices per square block than anywhere else in the city.

The noise of the choppers was muffled, but I witnessed a constant flow of traffic in and out of the city. I wondered where they all came from and what kinds of trauma or sickness they carried. This thought plagued me during lunch. Frequently, I whispered a prayer for the passengers of the helicopters as well as for the families of the patients.

Despite all the activity from ambulances and medical helicopters, I was enjoying a peaceful and quiet lunch with my children. Suddenly, I was drawn to a middle-aged woman who had just walked through the door of the restaurant. She sat in the booth directly in front of the one we were sitting in. This woman joined a man who had been sitting there with his back to us. As the woman sat down, she faced me. I saw many emotions on her face. Fear seemed to be the dominant expression, but I also saw pain, dread and anxiety. These emotions flickered across her features like scenes from a horror movie. Her body language portrayed her anxiety, and I could see that she was dealing with some type of devastating news. As I watched her, I heard God speak these words: "Tell her it will be all right. I'm with her. Tell her that you will be praying for her."

During the rest of lunch, I argued with God and myself. "Was that You, God?" I asked. When I heard the words repeated, I knew that I had to be obedient to His voice. I wondered what this lady and her husband would think of a total stranger invading their private and painful conversation that day.

As my three children and I got up to leave, I stopped at her table, touched her arm and said, "God said to let you know that everything will be all right. He is with you. I will be praying for you and your family." Her astonished look turned quickly to tears as she dropped her head and whispered thank you. As I walked out of the restaurant, I glanced back to see her and her husband's heads bent together as they cried. I couldn't help but cry myself. I had absolutely no idea who was sick or possibly dying or what had caused the woman's sorrow. It didn't matter. What mattered that day was my obedience to the still, small voice of God. I realized with clarity in that moment that God was using me to be His hands, His feet, His eyes, and His voice. As His followers or as Christians, we are called to be obedient to His voice in order for Him to accomplish His purpose on earth.

During my few minutes of arguing with God, I really knew that it was God speaking to me and not some wild idea of my own. But I worried that the woman would think I was a crazy person when I started the conversation with, "God said. . . ." I was afraid that she would be angry that a stranger would interrupt her during a private moment. Quickly, I put these thoughts out of my mind realizing that Satan wanted me to sit back, shut my mouth, and ignore the voice of the Lord.

After I left the restaurant, I felt a peace for whatever the situation in the woman's life. To this day, I don't know what she had to live through or deal with. But I believe that her burden was somehow eased by the words that were given to her from a God who cared enough about her life to send her words of comfort at her moment of need.

God will use all of us, if we will allow Him, to help ease the pain and hardship of others. We are His mouthpiece, carrying His Word and His message to others. We are His hands and His feet as we help someone else in need. He will use all of us if we will learn to hear His voice and then be obedient to that voice.

For as by one man's disobedience many were made sinners, so by the obedience of one shall many be made righteous (Romans 5:19 KJV).

Mary

If the son (Christ) therefore shall make you free, ye shall be free indeed (John 8:36 KJV).

It was the fall of 2007. I was working the evening that Mary was brought into the emergency department. She was not breathing and barely had a pulse. The heroin was pulling her under and Mary was drifting into a subconscious state. As I watched the paramedics and ED staff work to save Mary, memories came to me of meeting Mary one evening while working with her mother.

It was four years earlier. Mary had called the unit for the sixth time that evening. She wanted her mother's opinion about what to wear to the Friday night formal at school. Mary was 14 years old but looked like an 18-year-old model. She was tall and slim with long, flowing brown curls. She had dark green eyes. She was becoming a beautiful young woman.

Mary had never known her father. Her mother's new boyfriend had recently become her step-dad. He was kind to her and treated her alright but something was always missing in their relationship. Maybe it was the strain between Mary and her mother that caused her new step-dad to keep his distance emotionally.

Mary really did try to get along with her mother. But there was never enough time for a conversation, a meal together or a ride in the car. There were always the distractions of her younger brother. Mary yearned for time to talk to her mom about the important things that were occurring in her life. Between her mother's two jobs, workouts at the gym and a new husband to take care of, there was never opportunity to talk.

All Mary wanted was for someone to care about what was going on in her life. Mary yearned to be hugged by her mother . . . to be told that she was loved. It used to be that way until her mom started working all the time. Then she met Mary's stepfather. Mary's mom began to leave the house early in the morning and not come home until late at night. Mary got nice things because her mom was working so much. She got name-brand clothes, all the latest electronic devices and money for whatever she wanted. The one thing that she wanted and didn't get was her mother's love and attention.

Mary began staying out past her curfew. She stayed away from her mom and her home for hours at a time. Mary spent many evenings with friends. She ate dinner with their families. She used to sit at the table and pretend that she was part of the family. Mary would have given up all of her money and things to have a real family relationship. It never happened.

Then Mary started running with the "wild crowd." She kept her own schedule. She went home on a rare occasion. Her grades fell and she began to miss a lot of school. Her mother really never noticed that she wasn't around until the school would call asking why Mary had not been there for days at a time. Mary missed so much school that she was forced to repeat her junior year.

The summer before she was to go back to school, Mary became pregnant. She was forced to quit school and move back into her mother's home. Life became difficult for Mary. The friends who allowed Mary to stay at their house told her she could no longer live with them. The father of her baby turned his back on her and told her to stay away.

Mary was forced to go back home and live with her estranged family. By this time, Mary had become an embarrassment to her mother, who seemed bent on making money and gaining social status. Mary stuck it out in her mother's house until after the birth of her son.

After Mary's baby was born, she and the child moved in with her grandmother. At first Mary was unsure about the move. Somewhere in her naïve consciousness, she still dreamed of having a real family with a mother who would be her best friend. It never happened. Mary had never been close with her grandmother so she was wary about moving into her home but she and her baby made the move because she had no where else to go.

During the first several months at her new home, Mary absorbed herself in the task of caring for her son. She didn't go out much. She helped her grandmother around the house and became the model mother to her little boy.

Then one day she ran into one of her old boy friends while shopping for food. She promised to go to one of his parties and that promise proved to be her downfall. She didn't realize what she was getting herself into by attending one innocent party.

While growing up, Mary's mom preached to her about the addictive properties of heroin and cocaine. These two drugs were especially prevalent in her hometown. Mary managed to avoid the drugs. She told her friends that she was too smart to get addicted to drugs. Even with the rejection of her mom, Mary still listened to her advice.

Now that Mary was older and had a child, she didn't feel the pressure to "get high" like she felt while attending school and running the streets of her hometown. Mary attended the party and enjoyed being around her friends again. At one point in the evening, Mary was talking with a group of people that she had known from high school. When someone passed around a joint, she decided it wouldn't hurt her so she took a hit and passed it on.

What Mary didn't know until later that evening was the joint had been laced with heroin. When Mary realized that this was a different high than what she had experienced in the past, she became angry and then scared. What if she became addicted? She had a baby to take care of. She could not fall into the trap of drug addiction.

A few days later, Mary could not stop thinking about the feelings of peace and euphoria that she had experienced at that party. She certainly didn't want to become an addict, but she was so tired of feeling the rejection of her family. She was tired of the lonely life that she led. Mary decided that any escape from her overwhelming existence would be a welcomed change.

Mary began to attend the parties regularly. She began taking heroin or any other drug that was offered to her. She had very little money to buy the drugs so she spaced out the time between hits. She was determined not to become an addict . . . a junkie. That determination was not enough to keep her free from the addictive properties of the heroin. Soon Mary needed the drug daily. She didn't have enough money to buy it and she was not able to hold a job. Mary ended up moving in with anyone that would help her get the next heroin fix.

By now her son was living between her grandmother's and her mother's houses. Mary was caught up in the heroin lifestyle. She wanted out but couldn't escape that addiction. Heroin was her only thought from the time that she awoke until she passed out from the next fix.

On that fateful evening in September when I saw Mary, she had been rudely awakened from her blissful, unconscious state. When paramedics gave her the Narcan (medication to reverse the Heroin effect) she awoke with pain and anxiety. This was caused by the lack of heroin in her system. Had it not been for the arrival of the paramedics and the Narcan, Mary would have died.

"If only they would have let me die," Mary said as she sat in the locked unit of the hospital. "How can I get over this addiction? How will I ever give my son a normal life? How will I take care of myself? Will I ever be free?"

These are the questions of many addicts in society today. The addicted are spurned by the rest of the community. Often labeled as bums or free loaders, the drug addicted wanders through life. They frequently have to beg or steal from others in order to get the next high. They don't care about food or shelter. It's the drug that dominates their wants and needs. The addict's lifestyle is not by choice. It may be that way in the beginning but most addicts eventually want to be free from the drug's controlling grip on their lives.

In Mary's case, the one thing she wanted most in life, her mothers love, was now further out of reach.

Mary's mom was embarrassed by Mary's life-style. She was now forced to be the primary caregiver for Mary's young son.

I wondered what would happen to Mary when she was released from the hospital. How much of a chance would she have to break free of her addiction to heroin? She had no support from her family. Her friends were few. What would happen to this intelligent beautiful girl who seemed to have it all until heroin took her life?

If the son (Christ) therefore shall make you free, ye shall be free indeed (John 8:36 KJV). This freedom talked about in the Bible includes freedom from drug addiction, alcoholism, pornography, gambling and any other thing that dominates a person's life. Sin causes bondage. Sin causes addictions, and addictions cause pain and heartache. Christ breaks addictions and gives us back our freedom. He gives us back our life.

Christ loves the sinner. He loves the addict. He asks us to do the same. As followers of Christ, we are to show love and compassion to those in bondage regardless of the addiction. Mary asked the question, "How do I escape this?" There is an answer. Christ can and will take away the addictions that control people and destroy their lives.

Tammie

And all things, whatsoever ye shall ask in prayer, believing, ye shall receive (Matthew 21:22 KJV).

Tammie has paralysis of her left side, the result of a stroke. The stroke occurred because of a ruptured cerebral aneurysm. The bleeding from the ruptured vessel caused irreversible brain damage, according to the medical experts. She is unable to use her left arm and she walks with the assistance of a leg brace. Tammie has been paralyzed for more than 11 years. In all of that time, Tammie has believed in a complete healing of her paralyzed state. She believes in a life after this one and knows that she will be free of the paralysis when she reaches heaven, but she also believes in a complete healing now . . . in this life.

The skeptics are many. She has heard people say, "Be thankful for what you have. Be thankful that you can still walk, talk, eat and remember." She is thankful but she also believes what the Word of God says. She believes the many scriptures that promise a complete healing by faith.

When the disciples encountered a demon possessed boy, they were unable to cast out the demon. Jesus came along and commanded the demons to leave. By speaking the words the boy was returned to normal health. The demons left and the boy had a complete mental and emotional healing.

The disciples had many questions about the futility of their effort to cast out the demons. They asked Jesus, "Why could we not command the demons to leave?" What they were asking was why they could not perform the same miracles that Jesus performed.

And Jesus said unto them, Because of your unbelief: for verily I say unto you, If ye have faith as a grain of mustard seed, ye shall say unto this mountain, Remove hence to yonder place; and it shall remove; and nothing shall be impossible unto you (Matthew 17:20 KJV).

Jesus doesn't say that a person needs great faith to perform the miraculous. He says that we only need a little faith . . . the size of a mustard seed. A mustard seed is one of the smallest seeds there is but when planted and given proper care, it will become a large tree with deep roots.

Christ tells us to take our "little faith," place it in good soil, water it and care for it properly. He tells us to take our seed of faith and continue to believe despite the circumstance or lack of change. He explains that our faith is like that mustard seed. We have to cultivate it. "So then faith cometh by hearing, and hearing by the word of God" (Romans 10:17 KJV).

Christ wants us to continue believing His promises. He tells us to stay encouraged even when we don't see change in our situation. He advises us to praise and worship him for the miracle that we so desire. He says, "Don't give up." In His Word (the Bible), Christ encourages us to continue to believe in order for our miracle to occur. It will happen in His timing.

Tammie still has paralysis of her left side but she believes that she will be healed completely despite what the medical experts say. Tammie says that she will not give up hope. Someday the paralysis will be gone and she will have normal movement of her left arm and leg. Even though it is hard for her to hang onto the promise of healing, Tammie continues to believe.

And all things, whatsoever ye shall ask in prayer, believing, ye shall receive (Matthew 21:22 KJV).

Addictions

Verily, verily, I say unto you, He that believeth on me, the works that I do shall he do also; and greater works than these shall he do; because I go unto my Father. And whatsoever ye shall ask in my name, that will I do, that the Father may be glorified in the Son. If ye shall ask any thing in my name, I will do it (John 14:12–14 KJV).

*A**ddicted! Mental illness!* The words conjure up exasperated, angry, and hopeless feelings. Many people have absolutely no patience for the addicted person, nor do they have patience with the person who is emotionally or mentally ill. There are those who see the drug or alcohol dependent individual as well as the mentally ill patient as weak, depressed, uncaring and a failure as a human being in society. Those who are not touched by addiction or mental illness many times feel disdain and frustration over people who can't put down the pill bottle, alcohol or needle. The very idea that these people can't keep a job, care for their children or maintain a normal relationship with those they love frequently causes anger and impatience in society today.

As part of my job, I am responsible to make rounds on all of the nursing units. This includes the substance abuse recovery unit as well as the psychiatric units. My nursing background in critical care and cardiology gave me occasion to see end-stage liver disease, cardiomyopathy (diseased heart muscle), massive infections and many other life-threatening diseases in people who have battled with drug and/or alcohol addiction for years. Many of the patients I cared for had physical health problems as a result of the drugs, alcohol and medications used to treat various mental illnesses. I've seen people at their lowest and worst state. I would care for those addicts and those with mental illness as I gave physical aid but I never really had to deal with their emotional issues. My philosophy was, "Leave that to the psychiatrists and psychiatric nurses who have the training. I'll take care of the physical needs, but let the experts handle the emotional and addiction issues."

Lately as I make rounds in these units, I have started to feel the pinpricks of guilt that God uses to get my attention. As I watch a man with an obsessive compulsive disorder (OCD) wash his raw and bleeding hands for the tenth time in less than an hour, or an autistic boy bang his head against the wall, or a heroin addict writhe in his bed with abdominal pain, I realize that God has given to me the very thing that these tortured souls need. They need Him. They need the peace, hope, freedom and healing that only He gives.

Many Bible stories talk about physically and emotionally ill people, who because of Christ's touch, were healed of their disease. These healings included people who were plagued with addictions, obsessive compulsive disorders, depression, epilepsy, schizophrenic disorders, fears and anxiety disorders.

The Bible talks about unclean and unhealthy spirits. In today's society this may include addictions to mind-altering drugs or substance abuse. Our psych or spiritual man is capable of developing illness or unhealthy behaviors. Addictions are only one example. Emotional illness, depression, anxiety, fears and phobias are all unhealthy psychiatric or emotional diseases or conditions. In Luke 8:21–35 is the story where Christ healed a man who lived in the tombs. It was said that he "had devils" for a long time. He didn't wear clothes and lived in the tombs or graveyard. The man himself came to Christ and begged him to stop the torment. Christ commanded the unclean spirits to leave the man; and in verse 35, it says that the man sat at the feet of Jesus clothed and in his right mind after he was healed.

As I sit and think about what "right mind" may mean, I have to believe that Christ is talking about a healing of the psych or spirit. Spiritual sanity, restoration, new man is how the Bible concordance explains the healing.

Christ performed healings and miracles time and time again during His short life on earth. In fact, it was the healings and miracles that attracted people. He became frustrated that the people came to Him just to experience the miracles and healings. His purpose on earth was to offer spiritual healing or a new way of life. But because of His compassion, He never stopped helping people who were sick. His main purpose on earth was to teach people a better way of life, a life of love, joy and peace with one another. He promoted the sacrificial, selfless, "give unto others" type of life. He tried to eradicate the selfish, "me first" lifestyle that permeated society back in His day. This same lifestyle prevails in our society today. Despite Christ's frustration over the fact that people flocked to Him for only their physical and emotional healing while ignoring the spiritual healing, He still felt compassion and healed those who were sick both physically and emotionally.

There is healing for mental and emotional illness as well as addictions. It is the same healing power fueled by faith and hope that is evident for physical healings and miracles. Christ did not just perform miracles while He lived as a human. He still performs miracles today.

Verily, verily, I say unto you, He that believeth on me, the works that I do shall he do also; and greater works than these shall he do; because I go unto my Father. And whatsoever ye shall ask in my name, that will I do, that the Father may be glorified in the Son. If ye shall ask any thing in my name, I will do it (John 14:12-14 KJV).

Christ tells us that the same power that allowed Him to provide emotional, mental and physical healing to people in His time is still available to us today. The most important point of the above scripture is that we must believe on Him and believe in the works (miracles, healings and deliverances) that He performed. I have seen heroin addicts accept Christ into their life, and the addiction is no longer there. Most in the health care profession know that breaking the addiction to heroin is nearly impossible. It happens very rarely. Just like the addiction to heroin, many mood and anxiety disorders are considered by society to be treatable, not curable. They are controllable with medication, but very few mental illnesses are considered to be curable. Christ proved that theory wrong when He healed many people of mental as well as physical illness.

And when he had called unto him his twelve disciples, he gave them power against unclean spirits, to cast them out, and to heal all manner of sickness and all manner of disease (Matthew 10:1 KJV).

Death

For as in Adam all die, even so in Christ shall all be made alive (1 Corinthians 15:22 KJV).

As I go about my nightly duties as nursing supervisor, I am frequently called to "pronounce" a terminally ill person who has just "ceased to breath." Death to the chronically ill or debilitated patient often comes as a relief from the pain and suffering that plagues those with a terminal illness. Because many diseases are deemed incurable, patients are often given a Do Not Resuscitate (DNR) or Comfort Measures Only (CMO) status. These patients are choosing to die with dignity. That means no bone crushing CPR and no mechanical ventilation or breathing tube. It means no kidney dialysis and no intravenous medications that help to make the heart beat normally. It also means no electrical charge to get the heart shocked back to a normal rhythm.

As I enter the room to pronounce a person who has died, I am always reminded of the stories of Christ. He would speak the words "get up" to the deceased and they would rise up and live again. When I walk into a room to pronounce those patients who have ceased to breathe, I sometimes pray for a miraculous return of life according to God's will. I also pray for the family who has been left behind.

Last night I was asked to pronounce an elderly woman minutes after the staff discovered that she had stopped breathing. I entered the room to find the woman's daughter and granddaughter at her bedside. After asking them to step out into the hall for a few minutes, I went over to the woman and assessed her for a pulse, respirations, response to a stimulus and pupil reaction. I always pray for the soul of the person that I am pronouncing even though I've always been told that the soul is no longer with the body after death. After looking at the woman closely, I could not pray the words that she be given back her life. Her jaundiced and swollen legs and arms seeped fluid. I saw her multiple bruises, the result of bleeding into tissue. It was evident that the woman had suffered before passing away and I asked myself, "Would she want to come back to the pain and suffering of this life again?" Looking at the woman's face, I glimpsed the faint and fleeting grimace of pain. The heart was silent and still but for two soft thuds that where heard during the first minute that I listened to her still chest. Breathing had stopped and the last vestiges of life were drifting away from her eerily quiet body. It seemed that I could sense her spirit leave the room.

I didn't pray for a miraculous return of life while pronouncing the patient. How much misery had she lived through? The suffering was enough that her daughter and granddaughter were ready to let her go. Looking at me after I walked into the hall, the woman's daughter said, "She is better off this way. She has no more pain and she has gone to a better place." Comments like these are frequently made of a patient who has died slowly from a terminal illness.

Writing stories about hope, healings and miracles from a nurse's viewpoint has made up most of my published material. Lately I've seen a lot of death and dying of many people with terminal illness. With most of my previous stories, I've written about hope for healing here in this life. Since the dying and death of a close friend recently, I feel compelled to write about the hope that extends beyond the short 70 (plus or minus) years assigned to each one of us. I've wrestled with the subject of faith and why my friend wasn't healed. I don't understand the ways of God. I don't understand why she wasn't healed. Did I not believe enough? Did I not have the faith? I'm still asking for answers for these questions and I may never know. I do know that there is more to a person's existence than the few years spent during this life. I do believe that there is much more of life after we leave this earthly place.

The parable or example of the seed is used to explain death and rebirth of those who believe in Christ. Everything that lives must die eventually. Everything dies but the seed which returns to the soil for a period of rest. It will then spring up with new life. Like the seasons, our life must be lived in phases. These seasons are described as the spring of birth or new life, the summer of growth and living, the autumn of dying and letting go, then the winter of death, sleep and rest. Nature is God's way of showing us that life is not over with death and the grave. Life does go on after our spirit leaves our sick and failed bodies. That life is reserved for those who believe in God and have accepted Christ as the Way to new life. *If in this life only we have hope in Christ, we are of all men most miserable (*1Corinthians 15:19 KJV).

Walls

For I know the thoughts that I think toward you, saith the Lord, thoughts of peace, and not of evil, to give you an expected end (Jeremiah 29:11 KJV).

The phone call and request came at 11 a.m. on a Monday morning. "Can you come over and talk about writing a book to the girls at the detention center?" asked my sister Bonnie, who was a staff member there. "One of the girls is leaving tomorrow, and she wants to know how to get a book published."

The juvenile detention center had opened about a year earlier and housed some 70-plus teens from around the state. The walls were block and there were not many windows in the place. In order to get to the classroom where I was to speak, I had to be escorted through two sets of locked doors. Entering the classroom, I saw the curious and guarded stares of the first 12 young girls. They were all dressed in gray. No jewelry. No make-up. No fashion designer clothes. They were all dressed the same. They wore gray sweat pants and gray sweat shirts that were much too big for them. They all smiled and called out hello. They were all a little wary of me, as I was of them. But they were anxious to talk to me about how they could put into words their own unique stories and poems.

Bonnie asked me to come to the detention center and talk to two groups of girls. I was to go into the classroom and speak to these girls about the act of writing and publishing a book. Each girl would get a personalized copy of a book that talks about hope and healing. They would then be encouraged to ask any questions they might have about writing.

Before I left to go over to the detention center, I prayed for words to say, realizing that this may be the only chance I would have to talk with some of these teenagers. They were girls who had suffered terrible things in their childhood and short adolescent lives. The following scripture came to my mind. *For I know the thoughts that I think toward you, saith the Lord, thoughts of peace, and not of evil, to give you an expected end* (Jeremiah 29:11 KJV).

Wondering how I could bring this scripture into a talk on writing books, I sat down with pen and paper and after praying for direction, began to write. Before long, I had two pages of words that talked about forgetting the past and having hope for the future—a good future that God has planned for each and every one of us.

After speaking to the girls, I handed each one a book. Many of the girls were poetry writers. Some were talented writers with powerful words and thoughts. Many of them said they wanted to write their life's story. We talked about hanging onto their dreams and persevering, despite the odds against them. Many of the girls were from the streets of Philadelphia. Others came from small towns and smaller cities in PA. These girls had seen murders, rapes and drug deals, and many had been sexually and physically abused. Many belonged to gangs. Some talked about the crimes that they had committed. Maybe they told me things to shock me. I don't know. Many of the things were said so nonchalantly that I wondered about all that these girls had seen and endured in their short lives.

We talked about hope in something better for the future. Most expressed that they couldn't wait to get out from behind these cement walls, but they also expressed fear about returning to the same environment from which they had come. The walls of poverty, drugs, violence and hopelessness seemed to pervade their lives.

Realizing that I had nothing to offer that would give them hope, I told them about Christ. I told them that they could have hope and peace despite their ugly past. I told them that Christ had a plan for each one of them. These plans were for good and not for the evil from which they had come. We then prayed together while the teacher and the guard looked on.

During my time in the classroom, most of the girls talked and acted like normal teenage girls. But in the 60 minutes that I was there, I heard stories of heartache, pain and rejection. These stories could have been read from a fictional work, not true-life experiences of children and adolescents. It is of little wonder that these girls act out their frustration, pain, and anger on society. They want help, and they want to be heard. I wonder, "Where are the people who caused their pain? These people included rapists, drug dealers, gang leaders, abusive guardians and so-called friends who pulled them into a criminal world at such a young age. Where are the parents of these girls?"

I was told by some of the girls that many parents don't care and have not written or called since their arrival to the facility. One after another told me their dreams and hopes for the future as well as the horrors of their past. I detected first the far-away, dreamy look in their eyes that was soon replaced with sadness, anger, and resignation of what their future will probably be when they go back home.

Sherry seemed like a confident, experienced young girl. She told me that she wanted to be a counselor and open a rehabilitation center for children. As she raised her hand to tell me of her dreams, I noticed the long, thin scars on her arms. Sherry was a cutter. Did she do it for attention? Did she cut and maim herself as a result of her low self esteem or her self-destructive state of mind? Was she sick with a mental illness that pulled her down into a pit of pain and despair?

Then there was Brenda. She sat with such a sad and confused look on her face. She didn't participate in any of the discussions until I started talking about the importance of reading. It was then that she tentatively raised her hand and said, "I want to read, but I can't ever remember anything that I just read." My heart went out to this girl who had obviously suffered in her schoolwork because of some type of learning disability. This disability prevented her from graduating school or getting a job.

Makala was leaving the facility the next day. She was going back to foster care and was going to live with a new family. She had lived with foster families before and had suffered at the hands of abusive foster parents and siblings. I only hope and pray that this new family will love her and accept her regardless of her past.

Last, there was Lisa, a young lady who told me how she had been raised by a minister grandfather. She told how he and she would go out on Sundays after church and feed the homeless. It was on one of these Sundays that she was abducted from the front of the church, taken into a Sunday school room and raped by one of the men in the church. Lisa was eight years of age when this happened. Her grandfather died soon after, and she had to go into foster care. Her mother was a drug addict and couldn't or wouldn't care for her. Lisa said that she grew up in church and loved God but couldn't understand why He'd allow her first to be raped then to be left alone after her grandfather passed away. She spoke with no emotion and had a blank stare during the telling of her past. I could tell that she'd told the story many times during her short life.

"What do I say to her?" was my question to God. Lisa was a self-mutilator who had dug a hole in her arm and frequently shoved items such as paper, pens, crayons, paper clips and anything else that would fit into this hole in her skin. When warned about the chance of infection and loss of limb, she would shrug and say, "I don't care. I want to die."

After spending two hours with the girls, I heard more horror stories than I could have ever imagined. I didn't know what else to do but say a prayer for the girls. I then encouraged them to write about or journal their stories, to express on paper their frustrations and anger. More importantly, I encouraged them to express their hopes and dreams. I told them that they may never find hope in the system or in other people, but there is always hope in Christ.

For I know the thoughts that I think toward you, saith the Lord, thoughts of peace, and not of evil, to give you an expected end (Jeremiah 29:11 KJV).

Charlie

Now we exhort you, brethren, warn them that are unruly, comfort the feebleminded, support the weak, be patient toward all me (1 Thessalonians 5:14 KJV).

What did Charlie do during his lifetime to make his daughter and two sisters hate him so much? They wouldn't acknowledge him even in death. Charlie's power of attorney was a brother in California. He wouldn't return the many hospital calls made to extract the name of a funeral home and location of a burial plot for Charlie.

Charlie's body remained in the morgue for six days before the hospital attorney and the nursing home where Charlie lived made the funeral arrangements themselves. His brother never acknowledged the telephone calls made to inform him of Charlie's death.

Maybe Charlie's estranged family feared that they would have to pay the cost of burial or cremation. Maybe Charlie just no longer existed in their minds and it was easier to pretend that he had died years ago. Whatever their reasons, an entire family chose to revoke all responsibility for lonely, demented, old Charlie.

Because he had served in one of the many wars that occurred during his lifetime, Charlie had a little assistance from the Veterans Administration. This, along with a meager $900 to his name, was what helped pay for the cremation of Charlie.

"Who will spread his ashes? Who will take the urn that holds all that is left of Charlie?" These are questions that I wonder about. Surely he did something good in his lifetime. He must have been liked by somebody.

Loneliness! It pervades the nursing homes, personal care facilities, geriatric psychiatric units and the hospitals of our towns and cities. Millions of people die a lonely, depressing death. We are a busy people. We don't have time for the likes of Charlie or grandparents or elderly aunts and uncles. Do we? Should we? These questions remind me of my neighbor and friend, Laurene.

I moved into Laurene's neighborhood 16 years ago. Her house is about ½ mile from mine and we live on a dirt road surrounded by acres of trees. With the exception of one more house and a camp, we are the only houses along the road.

Laurene has cared for both young and old during the years that I've known her. Laurene's mother and mother-in-law were both bedridden and over 90 years of age. As a home health nurse, I made daily visits for a while to care for the wounds of Laurene's mother-in-law. I used to leave the home thinking that Laurene should be given saint status. There are very few people who would take on the job of feeding, bathing, lifting and caring for the elderly.

For several years Laurene was unable to leave her home for a long period of time. If she went to the store or to a school event for one of her grandchildren, someone would have to come and stay with the elderly women.

One day I asked Laurene how she did it. She replied with the question, "What else would I do? I can't and won't put them in a home. It's my responsibility." Shrugging her shoulders she said, "I just do it."

There are not many people left in the world like Laurene. Not many people would put their own lives on hold to care for someone else's needs.

Comparing the life of Laurene's family as they lived their last few years being loved and cared for, with that of Charlie made me sad. Charlie died a demented old man who was loved and cared for by the nurses on the geriatric psych unit. These nurses, therapists and nursing assistants made Charlie's last few weeks of life less lonely and less isolated.

It was those last six days spent lying on a cold metal pan in the morgue with no one to claim ownership of what was left of a life lived, that spoke volumes about Charlie's loneliness.

No one knows what Charlie did to his daughter, brother and sisters who remained. Whatever it was, it warranted an unforgiving heart on their part even after his death. It makes me wonder if Charlie's family will truly be able to ever let go of the anger, bitterness, hurt or resentment that they had towards Charlie. Even though he's gone, without forgiveness, those destructive emotions will remain until their own death. These emotions may remain buried. They may never be acknowledged again but they will remain. The fact is, an unforgiving heart will not hurt Charlie any longer but it will remain like chains around the neck of his family who were unable or unwilling to forgive.

The destructive emotions of anger, bitterness, fear, resentment, jealousy, and hurt will not go away without forgiveness. With forgiveness, destructive emotions will no longer have a hold over a person's life.

Futility

Now unto him that is able to do exceeding, abundantly above all that we ask or think according to the power that worketh in us (Ephesians 3:20 KJV).

The ethics professor defined futility in this way: "No chance or no hope of reaching the goals set by either the patient or the family. No hope!"

"But there is always hope," countered one of the social workers involved in the discussion.

"There is no hope if there is not a chance of reaching the goal. The effort is futile," said the professor.

The discussion centered on the question, "Should physicians be permitted to withhold medical care of a patient who is deemed brain dead?"

The answer given by the experts was, "Yes, but only if the chance of recovery or return to life is impossible should the physician be permitted to withhold care. We all know that it is futile to expect a return to life if a patient is brain dead or has no electrical activity on his/her electroencephalogram (EEG)."

The social worker asked, "But what about the chance of a miracle for the patient?"

Around and around the discussion went. What was the right answer? The possibility of everybody in the group coming to a concrete conclusion was futile!

Driving home from the meeting, I tuned into the local Christian radio station. The topic of the speaker's lesson was, "Futility and how to overcome it." I wondered about the fact that I never hear the word "futility." Then today, I heard it defined and repeated many times by the ethicist and then this minister. For three hours I heard discussion about the conditions of futility.

In the Bible, John 21:1-7 tells the story of Peter, a fisherman by trade. Peter went out one night to fish. After an entire night of work, he caught no fish. He brought his boat and his crew onto the shore. After unloading the heavy nets, he began the arduous process of washing and cleaning them. Peter was probably frustrated and depressed after an entire night of fishing with nothing to show for his work. His work that night was futile . . . a waste of time and effort. Peter's work and effort were in vain. He definitely did not reach his goal of catching a lot of fish.

What a depressed feeling a futile effort causes. Peter might have asked, "What's the use?" He might have looked at his crew and said, "I quit!"

Peter must have had these feelings as he washed his nets. But as he was washing, Christ came along and told him to go back out and cast his nets on the right side of the boat. Now Peter probably wanted to ask, "What's the use?" He was an expert fisherman. He had been out the entire night. He and his men were exhausted. I'm sure that the last thing he wanted to do was go back out onto the sea. But Peter and the disciples did as they were commanded. They went back out and did as Christ told them. By obeying the voice of Christ, even after a night of futility, they were successful this time and caught a multitude of fish.

With Christ in the picture, the word "futility" does not exit. Christ is able to reverse any futile or hopeless situation. With Christ, there is always hope and anything is possible.

Freedom to Hope

If in this life only we have hope in Christ, we are of all men most miserable (1 Corinthians 15:19 KJV).

We live in a nation of fear, anxiety, depression and hopelessness. These negative, and many times, destructive emotions existed long before 9/11 but not to the degree that they exist today. Because of the united spirit of America that day in September, we have a renewal of hope. Many Americans placed their hope in the government. When the situation was overwhelming as it was on 9/11, people felt that the government let them down, and their hope was diminished. People felt exposed and unprotected. As we watched the selfless acts of many Americans during the days and weeks after the event, our hope was renewed. There was a resurgence of hope because of the united spirit of Americans.

Hope! We all have hope that we will not see another attack on our cities and people. We hope that war will end soon and there will not be another young American dead in Iraq. We hope for peace in our day-to-day existence.

Will we ever see peace again? Will we ever see the end of fear, mistrust and hatred of people? We ask these many questions to ourselves and others after watching or listening to the news headlines. Where is our hope?

Hope is what prevents us from giving up. I see suicide attempts every day that I work. Over the Labor Day weekend, I admitted three people who had decided that their life was not worth living any longer. These three people had lost all of their hope. The age range was 25 to 50. One of the young women had a 14-month-old child and had just gotten married. This was her third attempt. How do people find hope in this stressful and angry world?

For several years, I searched for some type of written pamphlet or small book to give to the families of pediatric and adult ICU patients. I saw such hopelessness, fear, anxiety and dread on the faces of those family members and friends of the ICU patient. They would sit day after day in the waiting room outside the unit. They would wait for some smidgen of news that would help ease their worry. As I would pass by while making rounds or checking on one of my cardiology clinic patients, I would look at the faces and feel drawn to give them something to help ease their anxiety. My words were never enough. Frequently, I would go into the unit and check on their loved one. As I offered either condition reports or encouragement, I felt like the words were being pulled out of my mouth so desperate were the family members to hear good news. I couldn't deliver the report fast enough. People wanted something to hang onto. They wanted just a little piece of information that would give them hope for that hour or that day.

The pamphlet or book was never found. Several years later, I found a paper in my Bible. On that paper were names of both pediatric and adult ICU patients that I had cared for over the years. They were names of people that I did not want to forget. I had written down the name, the age, the diagnosis and information that made that patient memorable to me. In most of the cases, a healing or a miracle had occurred. Nearly all of these patients should have died, but they didn't. The family, the medical team and all of the prayer warriors who had hope and exercised faith saw the patient live. Hope, accompanied by faith, allowed the child or adult to walk out of the ICU and go home to their family.

There are miracles that occur around us every day. Most people don't acknowledge them as miracles but as events of life. I encourage you to see them through your spiritual eyes and not just as physical events. Talk to those individuals who have survived cancer or bypass surgery. Listen to their words of hope and encouragement.

In many instances in life, a miracle occurs or a healing is provided. Sometimes, neither one will occur. Patients die. But death doesn't have to be frightening for these people who fail to see a miracle or healing. There are some patients and their loved ones who believe in something greater after this life. They have hope in God, who promises that there is life after death for those who believe. *If in this life only we have hope in Christ, we are of all men most miserable* (1 Corinthians 15:19 KJV).

Perhaps you have been involved in the death and dying of a loved one or a friend. Because of hope, patients who have been deemed terminal can look death in the face and be free of the fear and anxiety that accompanies death.

It is said that there are few people who remain atheists or agnostic on their death bed. I don't know if this is true. I do know that God gave us all hope and a measure of faith. What we do with this gift is up to us.

A few months ago, I spoke about hope to a group of cancer survivors. My words were just those . . . words. After hearing the stories of several brave women who had battled or were battling cancer, I understood true hope. These women were witness to what hope can do to the human spirit. They were a group of women who were in various stages of cancer. Some had survived and were cancer-free. There were a few who had just been diagnosed. Some of the women had been given a death sentence and had only months to live. None of them were hopeless. Those who were dying expressed a peace that could not come from anywhere but God. They had not given up hope. These dying women still had hope in a healing of their cancer, but they had accepted the fact that they might not live to see their children graduate from school. They might not hold their first grandson or attend their daughter's wedding. But they were not depressed or despondent. They were hopeful and full of faith. They were going to accept what the future held for them. Why? Because of a hope in Christ and what He can offer, these women were at peace.

It was hope that caused so many brave men and women to flock to New York City after the fall of the Twin Towers on September 11, 2001. These men and women held onto a hope that someone would still be alive, despite the atrocities all around them. After days, weeks, then months, the rescue workers continued to search for the living. Eventually, their search was in hope of finding some type of physical closure for the many families of the victims of 9/11.

There was senseless loss of life on September 11, 2001. But our nation rebounded and united together to ease the pain and loss of the victim's families. They united to work together to make life safer in the future. People continue to have hope despite the loss.

Without hope, we all die. People experience hope in different ways. Many people hope and pray when circumstances are difficult or overwhelming. Some people hope for things to turn out okay, but spend countless hours wondering, fretting or worrying. There are people who hope for a good end to a situation, but they really don't have the faith to believe that things will turn out the way they hope. There are numerous Bible scriptures that tell us that our hope is in the Lord. If we put our hope in Him, He will give us a measure of faith that will increase if we believe. This hope and faith is what allows us to see healings and miracles occur.

Regardless of where you place your hope, the human spirit can not continue without it. Hope is necessary for us in this life. There is a belief that people can will themselves to die. I have seen people who cling to life until their loved ones arrive or until a special event occurs. I have seen patients who give up and die after being told they have to go live in a long-term care facility. The multiple suicide attempts occur because people have given up. Depressed men and women take their own lives. Many people turn to drugs or alcohol to help ease the anxiety and fear in life. People who have failed to see their dreams become reality succumb to depression and apprehension because they lose hope.

Hope is not a tangible feeling or emotion. We can lose everything in life and still have hope. It rises out of the ashes of our pain, sorrow and disappointments. It allows us to face each new day. Without hope, nothing is possible! With hope, everything is possible!

Hell Night

*And because iniquity shall abound, the love of many shall wax cold (*Matthew 24:12 KJV*).*

The call came to me around 8 p.m. It was one hour after I started my shift. The Emergency Department (ED) secretary called to inform me that they were transferring a two-year-old sexual assault victim to the children's hospital in a city 60 miles away.

One of the duties of my job was to keep documentation of any transfers in and out of the hospital as well as any unusual events that occurred during my shift. As I wrote down the information on the two-year-old sexual assault victim, I had no idea how many "unusual events" I would encounter that night.

After hanging up the phone with the emergency department, one of the nurses on the medical surgical unit called and asked me to come and talk with one of the patients. The elderly man had been a patient for three days and was looking forward to discharge early the next day. As I walked into the room to talk with Mr. Fair, who was assigned the bed by the door, I heard swearing and shouting from the patient in the window bed. Mr. Fair looked at me and said, "They just moved him to that bed, and I have never heard such language from anyone in my life. Move me out in the hall if you have to, but I'm not staying in this room with that man."

As I tried to calm Mr. Fair and assure him that I'd find him a quieter room, Nick, the 82-year-old man in the window bed, began to kick and scream at the nursing assistant assigned to sit with him. I looked over to see the urinal and nurse call bell being thrown at the staff member. The objects bounced off the wall beside the nursing assistant. Even with the door closed, the yelling was so loud that it could be heard by everyone on the unit.

Trying to calm Nick, who was a psychotic, elderly gentleman from a nearby nursing home, proved fruitless. He looked back and forth at the three staff members who were attempting to keep him from harming himself and anybody else around him. His paranoia prevented him from hearing or understanding that we were there to help him and not hurt him. There was no reasoning with Nick that evening. The nurse got orders for sedation medication; and after about 30 minutes, Nick calmed down enough for the guards to leave the room.

Nick spit at the staff. He kicked or punched anyone who came within arm's length and it was hard to look at him and not get angry. I realized that it was not his fault. He was not in control of his actions. It was his sickness that was causing this behavior. Before the guards got out of his room, they were paged to the ED. The page required a stat (immediate) response.

I followed the guards to the ED. As I walked into the unit, I heard the overhead page for a code yellow. The code was being called because one of the ED patients was behaving in a manor that posed a threat to either him or others. Looking into bed 12 of the ED, I saw four security guards leaning over a stretcher that held a young man. The man was of medium size. There were two nursing personnel holding each leg and two nursing personnel holding each arm. A large paramedic was trying to keep the man down on the stretcher by holding onto his shoulders. A psychiatric case manager was attempting to reason with and calm the patient. Again, I heard yelling and swearing. This 19-year-old boy was out of control — the result of drugs and alcohol. The young man was not visible because of all the staff required to keep him confined to the stretcher and thus safe from harming himself and others. Even though the man was not seen, he was definitely heard. After being restrained, the young man was given sedation medication. He was verbally threatening death to each nurse, medic and security guard in the room.

The ability of this 19-year-old, 150 pound young man to move despite the nine people holding him down was the result of the drugs that he had taken. After he had been medicated and had calmed down slightly, the staff moved the man and the stretcher into a more private room off to the side of the ED. As he was wheeled past me, I saw the crazed look on his face. I looked at him and again realized that this behavior was the result of drugs that were controlling his thinking and his actions.

As I went from one unusual event to another, I prayed, "Let me make a difference, and use me to show people that there is a better way to deal with life's problems besides drugs and alcohol. That escape is in You, Lord. Amen."

As I walked out through the double doors, I heard a nurse shouting, "Someone help me with this kid! I can't tell if he's breathing." Following her back into the ED, I saw a young man in his early twenties slumped over in a wheelchair. Four of the ED staff lifted him onto a stretcher. He had passed out with vomitus covering his clothes. He reeked of alcohol. This 21-year-old had drunk so much alcohol that he was unconscious and barely breathing. He was treated for alcohol poisoning. The young man had arrived with the help of a friend who had dragged him into the ED, placed him in a wheelchair and took off out the front doors.

According to the ED staff, patients arrive this way frequently. The patient is usually a young person with a drug or alcohol overdose. Someone will bring the patient to the entrance, leave them at the triage desk and then take off. Many times, the patient is cyanotic (blue) and barely breathing. Such was the case with this young man. He was stimulated numerous times by the staff to take deep breaths. His alcohol level was at a toxic level.

While rounding on one of the psychiatric units, I was approached by a staff member who reported that one of the residents had attacked her and kicked her leg. She had suffered a previous injury in this leg and as a result had developed a blood clot. The patient who had kicked her was sitting in a chair, yelling out at people and attempting to kick or hit anyone who came near.

After returning to the office, I was again notified of a transfer out of the ED to a local trauma hospital. The 46-year-old woman had a diagnosis of multiple falls with bruises, a cerebral contusion and possible abdominal injury. The patient would not admit the cause, but it was determined that the injuries were the result of physical abuse.

Sitting at the desk, writing up one unusual event after another that night, I realized that God had given me a glimpse of what many people experience in life. Mental illness, drug and alcohol overdoses, psychosis, sexual and physical abuse, suicide, hatred and hopelessness are experienced by people all around us every day.

Reading from the Gospels earlier that day, I realized that Christ talked about evil spirits of sickness, addiction and psychosis. What had I witnessed that night? Was it the evil spirits that Christ referred to or were the abnormal patient behaviors the result of drugs, alcohol and disease? Whatever the cause, I am fearful of a society where people seem to have lost control of their actions and their emotions, a society where anything goes and everything is all right regardless of morals and values. It doesn't matter who else is hurt because of these emotions and actions. Talking about the last days, Christ said this, "And because iniquity shall abound, the love of many shall wax cold" (Matthew 24:12 KJV). I saw a lot of unusual things that night but I didn't witness a lot of love.

Love Thy Neighbor

Jesus answered, Verily, verily, I say unto thee, Except a man be born of water and of the Spirit, he cannot enter into the kingdom of God. That which is born of the flesh is flesh; and that which is born of the Spirit is spirit. Marvel not that I said unto thee, Ye must be born again (John 3:5-7 KJV).

Leathery, brown skin hung on his emaciated, bony body. The lone man stumbled past us as he made a concentrated effort to walk in a straight line. His eyes were half open, and it appeared to take every ounce of energy he had to remain on his feet. Maybe it was drugs or maybe it was alcohol that caused him to walk this way. It could be lack of sleep combined with poor nutrition that caused his weakened and slumberous state. I remember looking at him and wondering if he was homeless.

It was August and Ocean City, Maryland, was teaming with people. The motel signs all said, "No vacancy." It was peak season, and the boardwalk was crowded. People of all shapes, sizes, ages and mental states walked up and down the boardwalk all hours of the day and night. There were many people who were oblivious to anything or anybody around them. Such was the state of Joe. I don't think Joe knew where he was going. He just seemed to be jostled along with the masses of people who flocked to the amusement park, shops and eating establishments along the boardwalk.

At one point, I made eye contact with Joe. He walked by and briefly glanced up. Looking at me for only a second, he quickly turned his eyes downward. He seemed to avoid any and all contact with the people around him. No shoes, no shirt, and with just his brown swim trunks, he really didn't look out of place except that it was after 8 p.m. and the sun was going down. A breeze from the ocean caused people to put on their "Ocean City" hoodies. It wasn't cold, but it was cool enough for at least a shirt. Joe didn't have one.

Joe looked tired as he slowly walked up the boardwalk. He was attempting to fit in with the mass of tourists walking beside him. He appeared to be hungry as he stared at the various foods being eaten by the people. He seemed lonely but he also appeared to have an altered mental condition.

Soon I forgot about Joe, but the next morning as I biked around the peer, I saw him walking onto the beach with a mat. It looked as though he was exhausted as he stumbled down toward the water. He was carrying a thin khaki mat that whipped about in the wind. Joe laid the mat down in the sand at the far end of the beach. Collapsing onto the mat, he seemed to fall asleep immediately. I wondered if Joe had spent the night walking and wandering, and then came to the beach to sleep. The signs said, "No sleeping on the beach from 10 p.m. – 6 a.m." It was now 7 a.m. Again, I wondered if Joe was homeless.

In front of the spot where Joe had collapsed were four large sand sculptures. Each sculpture depicted a scene from the Bible. One was Noah with the ark and several animals. The second was Jesus praying in the garden prior to the crucifixion. The third was Jesus reclining with His friends at the table. The fourth was the face of Jesus and the words, "Love God first, then love others as yourself."

In all the years that I have been coming to this particular beach I've noticed that these sand sculptures seem to dominate this end of the beach and boardwalk. Ironically, the sand sculptures are created by an artist, a young man who was also a homeless wanderer. The man had lived a life filled with alcoholism, drug addiction and loneliness. He had attempted suicide by slicing his wrists, swallowing a large number of pills and finally by putting a gun in his mouth. Before he could pull the trigger, someone came along and gave him a way out of his messy life. This person gave him an escape from addiction and pain and into a way of life that brought joy and peace. A young Air Force recruiter told the artist about Jesus and the state of being reborn or changed. Jesus talked to Nicodemus in John chapter three about being changed, about being born of water and spirit, not of flesh.

The artist wanted out of his confused and painful life. He prayed a simple prayer of forgiveness of his sin or earthly ways and asked Jesus to come into his life. It was only a few short statements, a simple prayer really. But Christ immediately came into his heart, took away every addiction and turned him into a new man. This new man was free of his depression, his wish to die and his addiction to alcohol and drugs. He now had joy, and, most of all, peace in his spirit. This young artist is now a street minister and helps young and old who have the same problems that he used to have. He tells people about the hope that exists in a relationship with Jesus Christ. He witnesses to millions of people every year through his sand sculptures in Ocean City, Maryland. I wondered if Joe had ever met the artist.

I didn't see him again that week. But I wonder about him. I wonder where he'll spend the cold and icy winter. Where will he get his food and shelter when the tourists pack up and go home? That leads me to wonder how responsible I am as a Christian. What is my responsibility to people like Joe? Oh, I'm sure that I'll pray for him off and on during the coming months. But is that enough? Should I try and find this stranger and give him 20 dollars or

50 dollars? Should I buy him breakfast or dinner? Should I tell him about Christ and about a better way of life, or should I leave it up to the street preachers or the next Christian that comes along and feels "convicted" to do something to help Joe? These are questions that I ask myself all the time. I really don't know the answers to these complicated questions. I just know that God has a way of pricking my conscience and letting me know that I need to do something for someone. It's this feeling of urgency, and I know that I have to act. If I don't, then I'm going to suffer guilt. The Bible says, ". . . Verily I say unto you, Inasmuch as ye did it not to one of the least of these, ye did it not to me." (Matthew 25:45 KJV). The two great commandments tell us, "Jesus said unto him, Thou shalt love the Lord thy God with all thy heart, and with all thy soul, and with all thy mind. This is the first and great commandment. And the second is like unto it, Thou shalt love thy neighbour as thyself. On these two commandments hang all the law and the prophets" (Matthew 22:37-40 KJV).

My neighbor is the woman down the street, the man next door, the teenager sitting beside me in the coffee shop, the girl riding bikes in front of me, the boy riding the skateboard behind me and Joe.

So now what? I have one day left at the beach. I've made a promise to God. If He lets me see Joe again before I leave here tomorrow, I will show him love whether by giving him food or money or just someone to talk to. I'll be obedient and show him love as I've been commanded to do.

Someone once said that if people would obey these two great commandments on love, then they would obey the Ten Commandments, also. Wouldn't it be a different world if everyone would obey the Ten Commandments? Or how about if everyone obeyed the two greatest commandments on love? It's almost too hard to imagine.

The Valley

Yea, though I walk through the valley of the shadow of death, I will fear no evil: for thou art with me... (Psalm 23:4 KJV).

Most of us have walked or will walk through that "valley of the shadow of death" mentioned in the 23rd Psalm. Many have been there . . . more than once. That valley may be a terminal illness, a devastating or near-death experience or it may be the death of someone we love.

As a child and young adult, I used to think that the phrase "valley of the shadow of death" meant that someone close to me would die and that would put me in death's shadow. With the loss of a loved one, I would go through that valley in the shadow of a loved one's death.

Yea, though I walk through the valley of the shadow of death, I will fear no evil: for thou art with me (Psalm 23:4 KJV). This verse and the entire 23rd Psalm has been recited at every funeral that I have attended. I wondered at those words. Does it mean that I am in the shadow of death as I sit here mourning the loss of a loved one?

Over the years, I have seen an increase in the number of patients both young and old who are diagnosed with a terminal illness. Most often, the patient is given a diagnosis of cancer with metastasis. The majority of these brave souls choose surgery to cut away the tumor or to remove the diseased body part. Then chemotherapy and radiation are added to try and eliminate the deadly cancer cells that have spread or metastasized to other body organs. I realize that those who battle a terminal illness are walking through a valley in death's shadow. Death has not yet touched these people, but it hovers nearby, casting its morbid shadow over the person's life.

How brave a person is who stands at the brink of this valley, knowing that there is no where to go but through. There can be no turning back, no detour, if that person wants to get to the other side. There is no choice but to forge ahead and start the walk.

There are many who make it through this "valley of the shadow of death." They come out on the other side a victorious survivor. It is a lonely, and painful journey. But the 23rd Psalm makes the promise that they will not go alone. Christ will go with them.

". . . thou art with me; thy rod and thy staff they comfort me" (Psalm 23:4 KJV).

People who walk through this valley are never alone. God has promised that He is with anyone and everyone who walks through this valley. Most people who may never acknowledge God any time in their lives will call out to Him when they traverse the valley. There is no one else who can help. God is always near to hear their heart's cry. He is always near to give comfort and relief from the overwhelming pain of the "valley of the shadow of death."

Recently I attended a breast cancer survivor group meeting. The name of the support group is H.O.P.E., which stands for Heavens Open Pending Emergencies. As I stood in front of this group of women, I wondered about their valley experience. There were some in the group who were true survivors. Anet, the group leader, and Debbie, one of the speakers, talked about making it through the valley. To hear them speak, one would think that the valley was not such a bad place. Then they began to describe certain steps in their journey. At certain places in this valley, Deb said she didn't think that she could go any further. She was ready to quit. But her doctor and a group of encouragers helped her continue the journey, and she is now a cancer survivor of 12 years. Anet said that she is a stronger person. She is able to help those around her because of her own difficult journey through this valley.

As I peered out at the audience of women in various stages of breast cancer, I saw a few women who were sad. Some were fearful. Some seemed resigned to the journey that awaited them. Most of the group had a peaceful countenance. They had walked or were walking this difficult and painful valley depending on the Lord for their strength and comfort. Debbie and Anet both said that they had a close relationship with God because of the valley experience. They stated that they were stronger and more able to reach out and help those who were just beginning the journey or who were somewhere in that valley.

Thank God for the survivors who are ready and available to help those who are forced to walk through that valley. I can honestly say that in almost 30 years as a health care professional, I have never met anybody who having walked through this valley is not willing to help their fellow man get through the experience. Whether by a prayer, a phone call, a card, a letter or simply a hug or encouraging word, survivors are a wonderful source of strength to those who are going through the valley. Isn't that what we are all called to do? We are to love our neighbor as ourselves. What better way to show love than to help someone else who has a need . . . someone who needs your prayers and encouragement.

Changed

Judge not, that ye be not judge (St. Matthew 7:1 KJV).

Matthew had tattoos covering both arms and legs. There wasn't much of the skin on his back that wasn't covered with snakes and dragons. He had numerous rings up and down both ears. His nose, eyebrow and tongue were also pierced. When I first saw Matthew, I wondered why the conservative administrators of the long term care facility would tolerate all of the piercing and tattoos.

It didn't take me long to find out that Matthew was one of the kindest and most ambitious young men I'd ever met. He was courteous and helpful. The patients loved him and so did the other staff members. His appearance made no difference in the care he gave.

Matthew loved music and frequently told me about the latest band that he had gone to see. Heavy metal was his favorite type of music and Marilyn

Manson was his idol. Matthew usually wore a black t-shirt under his white uniform and sometimes pictures of a skull, bones or blood dripping from grotesque faces could be seen through his white uniform top. One day I asked Matthew why he chose to listen to music that was so dark and depressing. He just smiled and said, "To shock people."

There wasn't a mean bone in Matthew's body and I witnessed him crying unashamedly about one of his patients on many occasions. He hated meanness and cruelty. He also hated injustice. He was not afraid to come to me with any number of patient care problems or complaints. Matthew was a strong patient advocate and that is priceless in a facility where many elderly are placed then forgotten by family and friends.

Matthew was in nursing school and he used to come in to talk to me about some of his struggles with school and work. He would tease me about dating my daughter or one of my nieces after seeing pictures of them in my office. Matthew was considerably older so I frequently bantered back and forth with him about keeping his eyes off my pictures.

Matthew used to ask a lot of questions about God and the contemporary Christian music that I listened to. I in turn asked him about the music that he was so wrapped up in. We compared musicians and songs. We talked about the meaning behind the lyrics of today's music.

During the time that I worked with Matthew, my children as well as a large group of youth from my church were involved in a drama team. The group had scheduled a concert for the end of May and Matthew saw the flyer on my desk. He teased me one day and said, "I'm coming to the concert to meet your daughter." We laughed but I told him that I'd really like him to come to hear some good music . . . music with words about life and hope, not death and darkness. He told me that he'd be there.

On the night of the concert, I waited in the back until it was time to start the concert. I had just begun making my way into the church when I spotted Matthew standing outside the double doors of the church. I opened the door for him and invited him to come in. It was the first time that I had ever seen Matthew anxious and at a loss for words. He was not sure what to do and told me that he had never been inside a church before. I took his tattooed arm and led him down the aisle to the second row on the right side of the church. A friend of mine told me that he would save a seat for Matthew since I had to stay in the back of the church. This friend promised to help Matthew feel a little more comfortable about being in church.

As Matthew and I were walking down the aisle, one of the church ladies grabbed my arm and pulled me over to her seat. Whispering loud enough for Matthew to hear, she said, "Tell him to take his hat off. Hasn't he ever been in a church before? That is disrespectful!"

As I removed her hand from my arm I loudly whispered, "No! He has not ever been in a church before so how would he know?"

I was angry at the comment made by the woman. She had made a judgmental statement about Matthew. God immediately reminded me of my first impression and judgment of Matthew with all the tattoos and pierced body parts.

Matthew went to the altar that night and accepted Christ into his heart. He still had the same tattoos and pierced ears, tongue and eyebrow when I saw him at work the next Monday morning but he didn't even have to open his mouth to let me know that he was a different person. God had changed his heart. He wore a smile from ear to ear. During the next several days he asked me many questions about God and living right.

I learned my lesson with Matthew. It is so easy to judge a person by his appearance. That is not what God wants of us. He asks us to accept all people the way that they are. He expects us to do what we can to show them love and acceptance as well as a better way of life ... a life that exudes joy and peace. This joy and peace comes only from Christ.

Voices

*And when he putteth forth his own sheep, he goeth before them, and the sheep follow him: for they know his voice (*John 10:4 KJV*).*

As she walked by me in the hall that night, I had to do a double take. Her six-foot frame was covered by two extra large, blue hospital gowns. One opened in the back, and one opened in the front. She weighed in excess of 300 pounds. Her hair hung down her back and was coarse and gray in color. The baseball cap that she wore was pulled tightly onto her head and down over her brow. She had no teeth. Both of her legs were wrapped with gauze, and she moved slowly as if it hurt her to walk. As I looked at her in passing, she picked up her head long enough to glance my way then quickly put her head back down. Staring at the floor, she lumbered toward the long-term care unit of the hospital.

When she walked away from me, I thought to myself, "Why would anyone let themselves get to that point—no teeth, straggly hair, a man's baseball cap, and more than 300 pounds?"

As I asked myself that question, I heard these words. "People are beaten down. They are unloved. They feel worthless. They need your love, not your criticism."

There are times when I hear the still, small voice of Christ deep in my spirit. I say a prayer and ask Him why when certain things happen in life. Whether by His word, the words of a song, an inspired book or the words of someone else, I hear the answer to my questions. Sometimes, I hear His still, small voice. The answer doesn't always come immediately, but God almost always gives me an answer eventually.

As a Christian, I have learned that Christ is only a word or a prayer away. I have learned to depend on His presence at all times. I've been asked many times by nonbelievers, "How do you know it is God's voice? Maybe it is your own subconscious!"

Satan uses the hearing of voices with the emotionally disturbed, drug addicted, or with certain mental illnesses. There are people in psychiatric units, crack houses and on the streets of our cities who hear voices. These voices torment and direct these tortured souls to commit acts of violence against themselves and others.

A few years ago, I heard a man telling his life story. He said that he was rescued from the streets of New York City. He was a heroin addict who was dying with hepatitis A, B, C, and HIV. He said that he suffered from malnutrition and wandered the streets night and day. He talked to himself and to the many voices in his head. This man said that he heard screaming from one voice and constant swearing and cursing from another voice. He also heard a voice that told him to do destructive things to himself and those around him.

This homeless man became so sick that he passed out on the street. Someone found him barely alive. He was taken to a New York City hospital to die. He had no family, no friends and no one to care about him except the incessant voices in his head.

This man described awakening from a coma in the hospital, and for a brief few seconds, the voices had stopped. As soon as he opened his eyes, the screaming and swearing started again. He tells of hearing another quiet voice that he describes as a sweet, still, small voice. This voice overpowered all the rest of the voices. The words that he heard were, "The day that you call upon the name of the Lord is the day you will be saved."

Those words were heard above all the noise and confusion. In that moment, he remembered those same words from a former coworker. She had told him that he had only to call on the name of Jesus and he would be saved from the pain and misery that tormented him. The homeless man said that he opened his mouth and cried out, "Jesus! Help me, Jesus!"

Immediately, the screaming and swearing stopped. In fact the voices were gone at that instant.

This man said that for the first time in years, he felt at peace.

Today this ex-homeless man sings with an internationally known church choir in New York City. He gives his testimony of how Jesus spoke words of healing and comfort as he lay dying. It has been several years since he lay in that hospital bed full of confusion and pain. The pain and the voices that tormented him are now gone. In an instant, he no longer felt the desire for heroin. His addictions were gone as he called out the name of Jesus.

When I hear that still, small voice, it is for my instruction or benefit. It is an answer to my questions or my prayers. The book of St. John tells us that Christ is the shepherd, and His followers are His sheep. *And when he putteth forth his own sheep, he goeth before them, and the sheep follow him: for they know his voice* (John 10:4 KJV). *My sheep hear my voice, and I know them, and they follow me* (John 10:27 KJV).

It is Jesus who is speaking in this tenth chapter of John. He tells us that if we are His children or His followers, then we will know Him and we will know His voice.

It was that still, small voice directing me to love, not criticize those who are sick and poor, downtrodden, and unloved. I knew that Christ was speaking to me. It is not hard to know what to do in certain situations. The question "What would Jesus do?" should be the question Christians ask in every situation. The answer is always the same. He would show love either through kind words or demonstration. He would show love by serving. That is what we are all called to do. Imagine a world where people went out of their way to help and give to others.

A Mother's Hope

And whatsoever ye shall ask in my name, that will I do that the Father may be glorified in the son. If ye shall ask anything in my name, I will do it (John 14:13, 14 KJV).

A mother's love is a lot of things. It can be described with so many adjectives and attributes, but the one word that describes it best is the word "hope." A mother hopes for so many things during the life of her child. One example of this is the hope of healing or a miracle in the life of a sick and dying child. There is the hope for more time to see and live through the milestones of a child's life as in the case of a dying mom. In the case of my mom, I saw the hope that life influences would not corrupt her child's Christian upbringing. Then there is the hope for courage to face each one of life's difficulties as in the case of a mom who has lost one child and faces the possibility of losing another.

Hope is the wish or desire for something with a feeling of confident expectation. Hebrews says, "Now faith is the assurance of things hoped for, the conviction of things not seen" (Hebrews 11:1 KJV).

During the years I worked in the pediatric cardiology department at Texas Children's Hospital, I saw hope defined in the prayers of mothers. Mothers would stay by their child's bed, refusing to leave. Mothers slept in a recliner for days and sometimes weeks, refusing to leave except for meals or a shower. It was the hope, faith and persistence of their prayers in most situations that resulted in answered prayers.

I dare say that if you are a mom, regardless of your age, you still fervently pray and hope for your children. My mom still tells me to lock my doors, don't drive fast and wear my seatbelt just like I tell my teenager and college-aged children. It is the same advice my 22-year-old daughter now gives me.

As mothers, we hope for the best in our children's lives. We hope for success and physical and mental health. We hope for our children to obey the law and avoid addictions. We hope for good friends and a perfect mate. In most cases, we don't always get everything that we hope for. That doesn't mean we stop hoping for the best. As young mothers, we learn what it is to worry about someone else as passionately as our moms worried about us.

I have a 22-year-old daughter who worries about me and her father. She heard that her father took a head dive off of his motorcycle, and with a stern voice and finger in his face, she said, "You better start wearing your helmet." It is funny how we as mothers pass on that ability to not only worry, but to hope for the best in all situations.

Hope! Without it, there would be no faith; and without faith, we would exist only in our daily circumstances. Imagine having no expectation for something better in our lives. And if we can't hope for something better, then there is no reason to have the faith that it will be attained.

God has given us as mothers and daughters the gift of hope. Hope for a better future. Hope for a different outcome. Hope for a miracle. Then He gives us the gift of faith to believe, truly believe, that we can and will receive what we hope for. Finally, He gives us the gift of prayer to ask by faith and then receive.

And whatsoever ye shall ask in my name, that will I do that the Father may be glorified in the son. If ye shall ask anything in my name, I will do it (John 14:13, 14 KJV).

Ask and You Shall Receive

If ye abide in me, and my words abide in you ye shall ask what ye will, and it shall be done unto you (John 15:7 KJV).

One evening, I was caring for a young man who had suffered a stroke. It left his entire right side paralyzed. During our conversation, I found out that this man was a Christian who believed that God could and would restore his health. But in a five minute period, he made the following comments to me: "I know that God will heal me. I just don't know when. Some days, I just wish I could die. I can't go on living this way. I have faith, and I know it will be in God's timing. But why can't I just be healed now? I would like to kill myself and get it over with!"

St. John, chapters 14, 15 and 16, state that in order to receive answers to our prayers, we need to ask believing by faith, and if it is God's will, we will be healed. It is by this faith that we abide in

Christ and believe His Word. We have to take this faith concept and God's Word and make it part of our being. We can't just hear the Word and say we believe. We have to live His Word. By faith, we bear fruit or live, breathe and speak Christ. It is not our preaching but our living that shows that Christ truly abides in us. I can think of many people who preach to those around them, but they don't live a life filled with joy, peace and love (three examples of the fruit Christ talks about).

A minister told the story of a wealthy adult business man who gave his heart to the Lord. He invited his adult son and family to church. At church, everyone was smiles and showed Christ's love as they shook hands or hugged one another. They sang and worshipped, along with the music. They said amen to the pastor's comments during his sermon. They showed true "fruit" on that Sunday morning.

On Monday and the rest of the week when the wealthy man's son encountered some of those same Christian people, he saw different fruit displayed by these Sunday Christians. Complaining, gossiping, cheating, displays of anger and meanness, drunkenness, fighting and cursing were just a few of the fruits or behaviors displayed by these same "church people."

The son asked his dad, "What do I need this religion for? I see no difference in the way the Christian acts and the way the rest of the world acts with the exception of Sunday morning. It would be my guess that they weren't being real when I saw how they behaved on Sunday morning."

Our actions do speak louder than our words. Spirits of depression, hopelessness, anger, jealousy and bitterness prevent the spirit of peace, joy, love and patience from manifesting in our lives. *Doth a fountain send forth at the same place sweet water and bitter? Can the fig tree, my brethren, bear olive berries? Either a vine, figs? so can no fountain both yield salt water and fresh* (James 3:11,12 KJV).

If a person displays anger, depression, jealousy or hopelessness, can they also display joy, peace and love of God? They may try to bear both kinds of fruit, but they are not being real. If God truly lives in us, then He has control of our lives. If we abide in Him and He abides in us, then we should be exhibiting His fruits. Joy, peace, love, longsuffering (patience), gentleness, goodness, faith, meekness and temperance (self- control) are the fruits of the Spirit. These are the attributes of the true Christian.

Some of the works of the flesh are idolatry, witchcraft, hatred, adultery, fornication, uncleanness, strife, envy, murder, drunkenness, lasciviousness (impurity), variance (fighting), emulation, heresies, seditions and wrath. *". . . They which do such things shall not inherit the kingdom of God"* (Galatians 5:21 KJV).

It takes conscious effort to get the focus off of self and onto Christ and others who need our help. There is always someone worse off than me or you.

No matter how bad the situation or circumstance becomes, there is someone who has it worse. You have only to walk through a pediatric intensive care or oncology unit to realize that many innocent people suffer in this life. It is our duty or calling as a Christian to offer comfort and help to those less fortunate than ourselves. You cannot give of yourself to help others without being blessed by God for your efforts.

As I listened and tried to encourage the young man who had spent the last five years in a wheelchair, I tried to imagine how I would react or feel if I were in the same situation. Would I go out and help others who were in the same condition? Would I have enough faith to believe that God would really heal me and give me the ability to walk again? I hope that I would believe the scripture, *If ye abide in me, and my words abide in you ye shall ask what ye will, and it shall be done unto you* (John 15:7 KJV).

Attacks

I can do all things through Christ which strengtheneth me (Philippians 4:13 KJV).

All the confused, desperate and hurting people that I saw this past week as I walked through the various departments of the hospital where I work are etched in my memory as I write this. These people worry, cry and criticize. Some walk around with confusion and depression written on their face. Many ask, "What are we supposed to do?" No one seems to have the answer to their questions.

The saddest face that I remember is the minister of 30 years who recently confessed that he was minutes away from taking his own life with a lethal dose of prescription drugs. He felt that this overdose of pills would ease the pain that he was unable to rid himself of. This minister had chosen a life of work and devotion to God and had become so overwhelmed with the pressures of life around him that he saw no way out but blessed sleep from which he would never have to awaken.

What has happened to people? Why, as a nation of blessed people, are we in this predicament? This minister represents the masses of hurting, depressed and anxious people who cross our path every day.

After attending a prayer service one night, I wondered about my own sincerity to pray for others. It seemed like the actual prayer lasted 15 minutes while my complaints lasted 40 minutes. "Why am I here?" I asked myself. Two people spoke of miraculous healings. One of the miracles was that of a young man with multiple sclerosis. He was healed and is no longer bound by a fatal, debilitating neuromuscular disease. It was good news yet it did little to bolster my faith. As I prayed for the many cancer victims, I still felt a sense of hopelessness.

I prayed, "God, what is wrong? Why can't I keep my mind on You? Why don't I care enough for the hurting and sick people to spend time praying on their behalf?"

"What is happening to the Christians in our society?" I asked God. As Bible believers, we knew that this day would come. Satan and his angels are loosed on earth, and they are attacking God's people. Because Satan's time is limited, he is attacking especially hard. People are succumbing to his attacks. He gets people right at their most vulnerable point.

Where is our armor? Is it off temporarily? Is our shield too small? Is our sword nowhere to be found?

Are we defensive Christians cowering in the corner somewhere? Are we trying with everything just to survive the onslaught, and is our faith (shield) large enough to ward off the fiery darts of the enemy? Is our sword a part of us, and are we comfortable using it with authority and power?

Many questions come to my mind. I pray that I will go on the offensive and not cower in the corner somewhere, trying to ward off the many attacks of Satan. I want to go on the offensive and push Satan and his angels back through the gates of hell. Christ tells us to do just that: *". . . and upon this rock I will build my church; and the gates of hell shall not prevail against it"* (Matthew 16:18 KJV).

When Satan attacks, I want my shield of faith to be so large that I am not affected. I can press on, knowing that I can fight off anything thrown at me. With Christ on my side, I will win. Satan can only take from Christ's chosen children what they will allow him to take.

I can do all things through Christ which strengtheneth me (Philippians 4:13 KJV).

Hope

I would like to say that every patient that I have prayed over for healing was cured of their disease ... that every terminally ill person received a miraculous recovery ... that cancer, diabetes, CHF or infections didn't take the lives of those entrusted to my care. But many died! Many of those who were given a terminal diagnosis died! Once in awhile, a patient overcame incredible odds and lived. They are survivors. They beat the odds. These patients came off dialysis, regained sight, had the breathing tube removed, had their tracheotomy closed, woke up from a coma, walked again after being told they would never take another step and spoke again after losing the use of their vocal chords because of a tumor.

So who survives and who doesn't? As I look back over the years thinking about the many patients that I have cared for, I see no pattern that makes sense. Why would a popular and beautiful 18-year-old girl die from a simple pneumonia, yet a 48-year-old heroin dealer with the same diagnosis live?

It is beyond our understanding. There are times when we who believe in healing wonder if our prayers matter to anyone who has a need. We may feel defeated . . . ready to quit. Then we are asked to pray for a friend or family member who has developed a life-threatening or terminal disease. With hope and faith, we join together and pray in earnest.

Does God answer our prayers? Yes! Sometimes, it seems that He does not hear us, but God always answers. It is not necessarily the answer that we want or think is the best. It is not always the right time or the right place to our way of thinking. But God always answers.

I've cared for sick, hurting people who are praying for God to come down and take away their pain, suffering and sometimes their life. These people are ready for death and what comes next. They've made their peace with God, and they know that what awaits them after death is so much more glorious than their last days here. These dying souls have not given up hope. Their hope is in a life after death . . . eternal life in heaven. The friends and family of this sick and hurting patient pray for a miracle, a cure or a recovery from the current illness. They are frequently angry or upset that the patient doesn't want the same outcome.

So whose prayer does God answer? The friends and family who fail to see the patient healed say that their prayers are unanswered. The patient who is ready to die, who is tired of the pain and suffering of this life, may have his prayer answered when he passes from this life. It is difficult to talk to the family of the patient who has passed on . . . the patient who prayed for an end to suffering and pain. The family frequently does not understand that the patient is indeed ready to move from this life to the next. This family many times feels that God didn't hear their prayer. So whose prayer does God answer?

I am reminded of a young father who developed colon cancer and who fought valiantly to spend just a little more time with his young wife and two daughters. Every church prayer group for hundreds of miles around united together and prayed for the recovery of the young father. He refused to give up. He refused to accept the fact that God would not heal him. He lived two years, longer than the doctors predicted that he would. He got to see his two small children grow for those two years before he died. Was his prayer answered? Was my prayer for him answered? No! It wasn't answered the way I thought it should be. I remember being upset with God. My faith felt like it was gone. But as I prayed and asked God why He didn't heal the young father, I heard His still, small voice say, "It was his time."

As a prayer request came in for a friend of mine who had just been diagnosed with liver cancer, her relatives, church family and friends joined together for a period of fasting and prayer. It was Sue's third bout with the disease; and at age 48, she wasn't ready to hang it up. So we all prayed. I have to admit that I prayed, but my faith was not very strong. Knowing the odds of beating liver cancer, I prayed with much doubt. When Sue went into surgery for the third time, the supposed liver cancer was found to be in a gelatinous form, and the entire liquid-type tumor slid off the organ into the surgeon's hands. The surgeon later told the family that he had never seen anything like it. He said that everyone on the medical team believed that the nodule or tumor was cancerous. It was not. My friend is alive and well after seven years. She and those around her had their prayers answered.

I wish that I could stand here and tell you that all those who have hope and faith and pray with a sincere heart will see their loved ones or themselves healed. But you and I know that is not always the way of the Lord. There are many scriptures that talk about healing. The Bible promises that if we have the faith to believe, then all things are possible.

During the past 25-plus years as a nurse in cardiology and critical care, I have seen the miraculous. What a way to bolster faith! But when I pray in earnest for someone's healing and I have to stand back and watch them die, my faith fizzles away. I just can't understand the ways of the Lord. The Bible says that His ways are not our ways, and we will not always understand His ways. Even though it is hard to keep the faith and hope at certain times in life, that is what He is asking us to do.

Whatever the outcome of our prayers, Christ tells us to cling to hope. Hope defined is to want or wish for something with a feeling of confident expectation. *Now faith is the substance of things hoped for, the evidence of things not seen* (Hebrews 11:1 KJV).

What are you hoping for? Is it for a healing of a devastating disease, a financial miracle, or the return of a prodigal child? Whatever your prayer or your desire, Christ tells us to cling to hope. Don't stop praying! Don't give up on what you so desire to see come to pass.

I thank God for hope . . . not just hope in this life but hope in eternal life after these short 70-plus years are gone. I thank God not only for the hope in the eternal but also for the assurance that I am His. He has forgiven me and made me His child. He cares about all the things that concern me, and because of that, I have hope.

More than that, we rejoice in our sufferings, knowing that suffering produces endurance, and endurance produces character, and character produces hope, and hope does not put us to shame, because God's love has been poured into our hearts through the Holy Spirit who has been given to us. *Romans 5:3-5 (ESV).

* Holy Bible, English Standard Version, Copyright 2001 Crossway Bibles, a publishing ministry of Good News Publishers.

Redemption

For God so loved the world, that He gave His only begotten son, that whoever believes in Him shall not perish, but have eternal life John 3:16 (KJV).

God loves us and has a wonderful plan and purpose for our lives!

While speaking with His disciples Jesus said, "...I am come that they might have life, and that they might have it more abundantly." John 10:10 (KJV).

For all have sinned and come short of the glory of God Romans 3:23 (KJV).

For the wages of sin is death, but the gift of God is eternal life through Jesus Christ our Lord Romans 6:23 (KJV).

We are all sinners. We were born into sin because of Adam's disobedience to God. God tells us that our sins can be forgiven by accepting that Jesus Christ is Gods Son. This is faith.

We must accept by faith that Jesus died on a cross as the ultimate sacrifice for our sin. But death could not hold Him. He overcame death and the grave. He arose on the third day as witnessed by more than 500 people

The only way to experience Heaven and eternal life is through faith or belief in Jesus.

Jesus saith unto him, I am the way, the truth and the life; no man cometh unto the Father, but by me John 14:6 (KJV).

For whosoever shall call upon the name of the Lord shall be saved Romans 10:13 (KJV).

But God commendeth his love toward us, in that, while we were yet sinners, Christ died for us Romans 5:8 (KJV).

But as many as received him, to them He gave the right to become the sons of God, even to them that believe on His name John 1:12 (KJV).

For by grace are ye saved through faith; and that not of yourselves: it is the gift of God:

Not of works, lest any man should boast Ephesians 2:8-9 (KJV).

Behold, I stand at the door, and knock: if any man hear my voice, and open the door, I will come in to him, and will sup with him, and he with me Revelation 3:20 (KJV).

Jesus is the only way to God the Father.
Jesus is the only way to Heaven and eternal life.
Jesus died on the cross to pay the penalty for our sins.
Jesus rose from the dead on the third day.
Every man, woman and child is a sinner and upon confession of sin and faith in Jesus Christ, will be changed. The bible refers to this newness as being born again . . . starting all over as a new being in Christ.

That if thou shalt confess with thy mouth the Lord Jesus and shalt believe in thine heart that God hath raised Him from the dead, thou shalt be saved Romans 10:9 (KJV).

Prayer of Repentance

Lord Jesus, Thank you for dying on a cross for my sin. Thank you for rising from the dead on the third day. I believe that you are God's son; that you are the Way, the Truth and the Life. I believe that you are the only way to heaven and eternal life. As a step of faith, I open the door of my life and receive Jesus as my personal Lord and Savior. Thank you for forgiving my sins. Thank you for making me a new person. Thank you for giving me a chance to know you and to be assured eternal live. Show me your will for my life. Teach me your word, the Holy Bible and guide me with your Holy Spirit. Make me the person that you created me to be. In your name I pray. Amen

Printed in the United States
220040BV00003B/1/P